Welcome to the Book of Common Prayer

Welcome to the Book of Common Prayer

Vicki K. Black

MOREHOUSE PUBLISHING

Morehouse Publishing
4775 Linglestown Road
Harrisburg, PA 17112

Morehouse Publishing is an imprint of Church Publishing Incorporated

Quotations from The Book of Common Prayer *are taken from the 1979 version.*

Cover design by Corey Kent

Library of Congress Cataloging-in-Publication Data

Black, Vicki K.
  Welcome to the Book of common prayer / Vicki K. Black
    p. cm
  ISBN 10 : 0-0-8192-2130-9 (pbk.)
  ISBN 13 : 978-0-8192-2130-8 (pbk.)
  1. Episcopal Church. Book of common paryer (1979) 2. Episcopal Church — Liturgy—Texts—History and criticism. I. Title
  BX5945.B53 2005
  264'.03—dc22   2004029520

Printed in the United States of America

07   08   09   6   5   4   3

For Waneta Irene Gardner Wesner
beloved grandmother,
woman of prayer,
teacher of English

One of my clearest memories of my grandmother is a conversation we had sitting at a picnic table in the backyard of my grandparents' "Little House" on the windswept prairie of the family farm in Oklahoma. It took place during my preteen years, a formative time of struggling with questions of a budding faith in my life. Her example of living the gospel in her daily life had always been intriguing to me, and I was beginning to consider becoming a Christian myself. "But how do you know God exists?" I persisted. She looked at me thoughtfully. "God is as real to me as this table," she said with loving but firm conviction, thumping the worn cedar plank soundly with her finger. I believed her, and was baptized soon after. She and I have prayed for each other ever since, until her death in 2004.

This small book introducing a book of prayer is dedicated to her, and to all the men and women who not only come to know the God of Jesus Christ through their life of prayer, but who help open the doorway to God for others.

Contents

Discovering the Book of Common Prayer

An Introduction

It is a most invaluable part of that blessed "liberty wherewith Christ hath made us free," that in his worship different forms and usages may without offence be allowed, provided the substance of the Faith be kept entire; and that, in every Church, what cannot be clearly determined to belong to Doctrine must be referred to Discipline; and therefore, by common consent and authority, may be altered, abridged, enlarged, amended, or otherwise disposed of, as may seem most convenient for the edification of the people.

(*Preface to the 1789 Book of Common Prayer*, BCP 9)

In Pixar Studio's popular children's movie *Finding Nemo*, Nemo's father, a worried and protective clown fish named Marlin, is searching the ocean for his lost son, who has been captured by a scuba-diving dentist from Sydney and taken to live in an aquarium in his office. Marlin encounters many dangers in his lonely search, but also one faithful friend named Dory. When at last they discover the address of the dentist's office, they are directed to find the East Australian Current—that will take them where they want to go, they are told.

Gathering their courage, Marlin and Dory brave a swarm of stinging jellyfish and land in the current, finding themselves swiftly carried along amid a great celebratory parade of sea creatures. They

1

no longer have to spend so much energy swimming alone, making their own way in a vast ocean. An especially wise old sea turtle named Crush teaches them some of the important things they need to know at that point in their journey in order to grow and continue on. By the time the current has carried them to Sydney and Marlin and Dory leap out, they are changed fish. Their fears have been replaced by joyful hope and their isolation by the caring support of a diverse community.

For many new Episcopalians, Marlin's experience of the East Australian Current echoes their experience of entering the liturgical life of prayer and worship in the church. Many of us have searched for God on our own for years, praying by ourselves, perhaps sharing our yearnings with a few faithful friends or perhaps being completely alone. And yet when we make the leap into the church's ongoing liturgical life, it is like suddenly discovering that a vibrant, powerful stream of worship and praise to God has been going on for centuries upon centuries. We are at first swept off our feet, perhaps a bit confused and uncertain. But soon we catch the rhythm; we begin to understand what is happening at each celebration of the Eucharist, at every baptism, at each service of Morning Prayer. We grow from the wisdom of the learned and saintly among us. And we discover we have been welcomed into an enormous, eternal, diverse community of human beings who are likewise seeking to worship the God who created all things, who is beyond all things, and yet who lives among us. We discover we are not alone, and this liturgical current of worship, prayer, and praise will indeed take us where we want to go—to union with the God we seek to love.

WHAT IS A PRAYER BOOK?

When you visit an Episcopal church for the first time, you will quickly notice that the worship service follows a particular order. The bulletin may direct you to a number of different pages in a book in the pew. Or the entire service may be printed in a leaflet, to help you avoid the confusion of finding your way in the various books. As you come back in the following weeks, you will notice that the service does not change all that much from Sunday to Sunday. You might see small variations here and there—different prayers and Scripture readings and hymns—but the basic form of the service remains the same. That's because in the Episcopal Church our faith in God is expressed, shaped, and formed by the rites for worship found in the Book of Common Prayer.

In the Anglican tradition (of which the Episcopal Church is a part), our prayer book is primarily a book of prayers and liturgical rites for public worship, though it may also contain devotions for private or family use. We call our prayer book the Book of Common Prayer: it is "common" because it contains the fixed texts of the regular services of the church, those used for public or common worship. It is also "common" because it uses the vernacular language spoken by most of the people who are using that particular book, rather than a specialized "religious" language, such as Latin or Hebrew. At the time of the Protestant Reformation, when our first prayer book was written, the term "common" may also have been used as a way of contrasting this book with the private devotional manuals used by medieval clergy and not available to the "common" people during worship.[1]

While called a "prayer" book, the Book of Common Prayer contains more than just prayers. There are also instructions for how to do the liturgies (called "rubrics"), biblical passages and a lectionary that lists the Scripture readings for the year, statements of beliefs called "creeds," and the texts of songs called "canticles." In addition to the well-known services of Eucharist, baptism, and Morning and Evening Prayer, the prayer book also includes the liturgies for less frequent services such as weddings, ordinations, and funerals. Having all of the texts for public worship in one book has been a part of our liturgical tradition from the earliest editions of the Book of Common Prayer.

The 1979 revision of the American prayer book also includes historical documents and a catechism—the basics of our faith in question-and-answer format. In many ways, the Book of Common Prayer defines and sets forth the faith and teachings of the Episcopal Church. Instead of spelling out our doctrines in a formal teaching document, we Episcopalians prefer to pray our way to belief. This way of moving from prayer to belief and back again is expressed in a Latin phrase, *lex orandi, lex credendi*—the law of prayer is the law of belief. In other words, our praying shapes our believing and our believing shapes our prayer.

Many Christian communities and denominations choose not to have a prayer book guiding their worship, but prefer the spontaneity of composing a different order for worship every week. We Episcopalians, on the other hand, find a sense of unity in shared liturgical texts for all congregations, in all situations, used throughout the nation—though the ways those rites are expressed in worship vary considerably from one congregation to another. We believe our worship needs to be "in common" and a part of the ancient liturgical traditions of the church: it is our way of living within the rich tradition of Christian worship, as we speak the words and do the liturgical rites prayed by Christians for centuries. Prayer book worship is part of our identity, and therefore is the foundation that binds the Anglican Communion together.

At the time of the Reformation, strict conformity to the actual texts used in worship was a matter of utmost importance because the church was "established"—intricately linked to the political rulers of the realm. As Louis Weil and Charles Price note in their classic *Liturgy for Living*:

> Refusal to abide by the authorized liturgy could be taken to mean theological heterodoxy or even political infidelity. . . . The invention of printing in 1440 opened the way to a liturgical conformity that could never have been demanded as long as only handwritten manuscripts were available.[2]

We live in a very different time, of course, and we have much greater flexibility in the liturgies available to us in the Book of Common Prayer. Our words and patterns of worship as Anglicans are no longer a matter of strict conformity and are not linked to our political affiliations; rather, they are the common ground of prayer from which we share in the Christian life. It is a remarkable experience to travel to different Anglican churches and discover that you are "home" wherever you are: the prayers and style of worship may be somewhat different, but the basic liturgical patterns and many of the words are familiar. It is even more remarkable to recall that some form of these liturgies has been used by Christians for centuries.

PRAYER BOOK ORIGINS

The Book of Common Prayer used in your parish church today was authorized in 1979, but it follows a 450-year tradition of worship books in the Anglican Church. The reformers in England at the time of the Reformation, including Thomas Cranmer, the archbishop of Canterbury, wanted the church's public worship to be available not only to the clergy and liturgical ministers, but to everyone in the congregation. The first Book of Common Prayer, published in 1549, established this norm, and it has been a hallmark of Anglicanism ever since.

To understand the history of this first Book of Common Prayer, however, we must begin not with Thomas Cranmer and the Reformation, but with the early church. For when Cranmer and his committee of bishops and theologians sat down to write an English prayer book, they did not start from scratch. Rather, they drew on many different sources: the ancient prayers the church had been using since its beginnings in Judaism, the Roman Catholic and Orthodox liturgical traditions, the elaborate rituals that marked the church's common worship and private devotions in the Middle Ages, as well as the emerging rites and prayers from the Reformed traditions in Europe.

Although we have very few liturgical texts dating from the time of the early church, the origins of Christian worship are found in Judaism, and reflect the customs of the Jewish Christians who lived in the years immediately after Jesus' death and resurrection. Jews were accustomed to praying at certain times throughout the day— morning, noon, and evening. The earliest Christians continued and adapted this practice, and over the next few centuries it developed into what we call the Daily Office. As in our offices of Morning and Evening Prayer, the psalms and other biblical songs were likewise significant in the prayer life both of Jesus and the early Christians. All Jewish meals were accompanied by prayers and thanksgivings, and our Holy Eucharist of bread and wine is rooted in this tradition.

Christian baptism too is adapted from the Jewish ritual customs of Jesus' time, as we see, for example, in the gospel stories of the crowds who traveled to the wilderness to be baptized by John in the river Jordan.

During the next few centuries, written liturgical texts known as "church orders" began to appear. They are collections of prayers, teachings, and liturgical rites that express the worship practices of a particular location at a particular time. These texts claim to be materials handed down from the apostolic age, as their names imply: the set of texts called *Apostolic Tradition*, for example, contains the early liturgical traditions from the church in Rome, while *Apostolic Constitutions* collects those from the church in Syria. These church orders are not prayer books as we know them; rather, their prayers and rites probably served as models for the liturgical prayers church leaders would freely compose during worship.

The next step in the early development of the Book of Common Prayer was the emergence of books called "sacramentaries," which were collections of prayers that could be used in the liturgy by the celebrant or leaders of worship. Since these were written prayers that would have been used regularly, they are more similar to our prayer book than the church orders, but their use was limited to the leaders of worship.

Between the sixth and ninth centuries the church developed the basic liturgical forms that we use today. For those of us living in the churches that originated in western Europe, the Roman rite is the foundation for most of our prayers and liturgies. Many of the collects (prayers with a fixed form—address, petition, and conclusion) in the 1979 Book of Common Prayer, for example, are drawn from a book called the *Leonine Sacramentary* dating from the early sixth century.[3]

Other texts for worship also emerged during the early Middle Ages: books containing the readings from the New Testament epistles and gospels used during worship, books of music chants for the choir, books of rules and directions for how to do the liturgies. Most were composed in monastic communities, where prayer and worship were a part of the daily routine of the monks and nuns. Beginning in the ninth century, these books were collected into a single volume called the *Missal*. In addition, books were needed for the Daily Office, containing the prayers, psalms, canticles, Scripture lessons, and readings from the lives of the saints that would be used for the hours of prayer throughout the day. These books were consolidated into a four-volume *Breviary*, as well as into a single-volume *Book of Hours*.

Other liturgical texts were also developed in the early medieval church, including the prayers and liturgies for services called the pastoral offices, such as marriage, baptism, burial, and visitation of the sick. These texts were collected in a book called the *Manual*, and the services specifically used by the bishop were collected in a book called the *Pontifical*. Finally, a book of rubrics, or directions, for all of these rites was compiled; it was called the *Pie*.

Thus by the eve of the Reformation an abundance of liturgical books, almost all for the clergy and monastics, had emerged in the church. Since the books varied according to the liturgical practices and customs followed in different locales, they provided a wealth of materials on which reformers like Thomas Cranmer could draw.

WHY A REFORMATION?

In order to understand the origins of the Book of Common Prayer we have to first understand why such a book was needed. At first glance it might seem that the Book of Common Prayer is simply a compilation of all the books used in the medieval church into a single volume; looking deeper, we find it is a book formed by the principles of the sixteenth-century Reformation. So we must first look at the practices and traditions that prompted the need for "reformation" of the church's liturgy, practices that the liturgical scholar Dom Gregory Dix has called the "deformation" of the liturgy.[4] To do that, we need to look again at the history of the Christian church.

When the emperor Constantine adopted Christianity as the official religion of the Roman Empire early in the fourth century C.E., the church suddenly was transformed from an outlawed sect marked by persecution and secret gatherings for worship in the homes of Christians to an established and popular religion with enormous wealth at its disposal. In the following centuries, Christian liturgies became elaborate ceremonies in stately buildings, where it was difficult to hear the words of the service and the distant lay participants grew increasingly passive and silent. Worship also became more standardized and controlled as the church developed a hierarchical system of oversight.

With the fall of the Roman Empire and the societal upheavals and traumas of the early Middle Ages, the piety of the medieval church became increasingly penitential. The focus shifted from Christ's triumph over death in the resurrection to his suffering and death and to human sin and moral purity, with seemingly little confidence in Christ's justification of all people. The social and political turmoil made it difficult to sustain the abundant joy and thanksgiving of all the people in the celebration of the weekly Eucharist.

As people troubled by an unrelieved sense of unworthiness, fear, and guilt shied away from receiving the bread and wine of the Eucharist, the liturgy became primarily the activity of the clergy. A distorted understanding of the Eucharist as in some way supplementary to Christ's once-and-for-all sacrifice on the cross led to a popular theology that "the priest sacrifices Christ afresh at every mass."[5] And with the words of the liturgy continuing in Latin long past the time most people could speak or even understand it, medieval Christians in the pews simply said their own private prayers while the priest quietly celebrated the eucharistic liturgy at the altar. A Christian from the early church would find these masses hard to recognize as a Eucharist.

A similar "deformation" occurred in baptism. As the Roman Empire extended to the tribes of northern Europe, entire households were baptized with little preparation in the faith—a very different experience from the early church's "catechumenate," the extended period of study and prayer before baptism. With the wholesale baptism of the people of entire countries, the only candidates for baptism left were infants. Infant baptism became the norm, and with the high rate of infant mortality, baptisms were done as quickly as possible. So the custom developed that baptisms should be done within eight days of the birth, effectively moving baptisms from the Easter celebrations in the church's liturgy to private services done throughout the year.

Clearly, by the late Middle Ages the worship and theology of the church, especially in the West, had lost touch both with its origins in the early church and with ordinary people in the congregations. When this was coupled with a new intellectual resurgence that often found itself at odds with the church's teachings and with church leaders, the stage was set for a major reforming of the church. Voices both within the church and outside its structures spoke of discontent with liturgy and worship and with the closed attitudes of bishops and other church leaders. More and more people wanted their faith and worship expressed in language they could understand and speak.

The invention of the printing press made it possible for information and opinions to be widely available and made challenges to church leaders more public. It was also now possible to place the Bible in the hands of ordinary people who were able read it. With William Tyndale's translation of the New Testament into English in 1524, English-speaking Christians began to rediscover the Bible. By 1543 the leaders of the church in England had authorized "the reading of 'one chapter in English without exposition'"[6] during the liturgy. Hearing the Bible read in English instead of Latin paved the way for prayers in English as well, and some churches experimented with drafts of the services in English that were later included in the first prayer book.

THE FIRST BOOK OF COMMON PRAYER

The first Book of Common Prayer was published in March 1549, during the reign of Edward VI, the son of Henry VIII. The archbishop of Canterbury, Thomas Cranmer, was probably the primary author and compiler of the book, but a number of other church leaders contributed to it. Cranmer's committee of twelve of "the most learned and discreet bishops, and other learned men"[7] met in the fall of 1548 and produced a proposed prayer book within three weeks. They could do so in such a short time because a number of drafts of the various parts of the prayer book—Matins and Evensong, an Order of Communion, the Litany, the readings from the Epistles and Gospels, and the services for baptism, burial, and marriage—were already in print. The principal issue of contention was the liturgy for the Eucharist.

On January 21, 1549, the Houses of Parliament passed the Act of Uniformity, making the Book of Common Prayer the official prayer book of the realm. Those of us who are still using this Book of Common Prayer eight revisions later know only too well that changes in liturgy bring dissension and conflict as well as renewal and fresh insights. Some in the church will enthusiastically embrace the new rites; others will go along with the revisions and quickly adapt; still others will find the changes intolerable and choose to fight or leave. As historian William Sydnor has noted:

> For each of those eight times, as well as for the issuing of this first Book, the occasion has been one of joy or anguish, relief or disgust, pride or dismay, dedication or revolt. In 1549, such strong feelings as these poured over the Book almost before the ink was dry.[8]

In the Episcopal Church today our quarrels over liturgy tend to be limited to bitter words exchanged within the church; in sixteenth-century England, opposition to the prayer book, which often turned violent, was inextricably linked to opposition to the government. The stance of the more conservative members of the church was stated succinctly by Christians in England's West Country:

> We demand the restoration of the Mass in Latin without any to communicate, and the Reservation of the Blessed Sacrament: Communion in one kind, and only at Easter: greater facilities for Baptism: the restoration of the old ceremonies—Holy-bread and Holywater, Images, Palms, and Ashes. We will not receive the new service, because it is but like a Christmas game; but we will have our old service of Mattins, Mass, Evensong and processions in Latin, not in English.[9]

This kind of resistance was met with governmental force, including execution. Those who resisted the new prayer book less violently simply continued to use the old Mass, despite the government's rigorous effort toward uniformity.

PRAYER BOOK REFORM

Almost before it was published, calls for reform of the Book of Common Prayer were being made from both ends of the spectrum. Conservatives wanted a restoration of the old services in Latin; reformers wanted even more innovation and clearing away of the medieval accumulations. English reformers such as bishops John Hooper and Nicholas Ridley and more radical reformers from Europe, including Martin Bucer and Peter Martyr, had become increasingly influential in England in the mid-sixteenth century. It is therefore no surprise that the revised prayer book that emerged in 1552 under the oversight of Queen Elizabeth I reflected their more radical Reformation principles and theology. A series of revisions were made to the prayer book in the century after it was first compiled, usually in conjunction with the ushering in of a new English monarch.

With the revision of the English Book of Common Prayer in 1662 under King Charles II, the church in England solidified its moderate position between the Puritans on the one hand and the more Catholic high church party on the other. Charles restored prayer book worship to England after the decade of Presbyterianism under Oliver Cromwell, and his 1662 Book of Common Prayer has provided the basis for subsequent revisions throughout the Anglican Communion. In England itself, it is still the official prayer book, despite repeated efforts to approve a revision. However, efforts toward revision in 1668 and 1689 were published and widely used, and supplementary liturgies have likewise been approved in recent years and are much in use.

AN AMERICAN PRAYER BOOK

The process of revision of the Book of Common Prayer continues to be fraught with conflict, frustration, and bitter division. The historian William Sydnor puts it well:

> A characteristic of some Prayer Book worshippers seems to be that often their attachment to the services and ceremonies with which they are familiar is so great that they consider them the ultimate and final expression of Prayer Book worship, the end of liturgical history.[10]

Though the Anglicans who made the journey to the new world and who, after 1776, found themselves in a new country were equally attached to the familiar "services and ceremonies" of the Book of Common Prayer, they knew it was imperative to create an American prayer book for an American church.

In 1786 leaders of this new Episcopal Church in America, including Samuel Seabury (our first bishop), William White of Philadelphia, and William Smith of Maryland, produced a revision of the Book of Common Prayer. This "proposed book" stated that it was intended for "trial use"—a method for revision that a number of Anglican churches would later adopt, including our own Episcopal Church in the 1970s. After three years of use in parishes, and following much discussion, dissension, encouragement, and further revision, the Philadelphia Convention of 1789 authorized a committee to oversee the printing of the prayer book approved by the convention.

Perhaps the most significant liturgical change in the 1789 prayer book was the inclusion of parts of the Scottish eucharistic prayer (the prayer of thanksgiving and consecration that is said over the bread and wine of communion).[11] This prayer from the Scottish Communion Office of 1764, with its emphasis on the offering of bread and wine and the invocation of the Holy Spirit to sanctify that offering, had roots in the liturgies of the Eastern church and in the prayer books of 1549 and 1637. The 1789 Book of Common Prayer was a fairly radical revision of the 1662 prayer book. It modernized much of the language of the prayers and included material from subsequent proposed revisions to the 1662 book. It also included material from other sources, such as Jeremy Taylor's popular devotional manual called *The Rule and Exercises of Holy Dying*, a notebook kept by Bishop Seabury, and the proposals made by conventions held in several states of the new country.

Perhaps the most significant non-liturgical contribution the 1789 prayer book made was to separate liturgical reform and prayer book revision from the political realm. Previous revisions were linked to a change in governance; now the church was free to revise its liturgies according to its own needs and desires. Though the 1789 book was prompted by the creation of a new nation and the need to revise the prayers for the monarchy, it became clear to the revisers that they had entered a new era in this new world. As they note in the preface to their prayer book, those meeting in convention

> "could not but, with gratitude to God, embrace the happy occasion which was offered to them (uninfluenced and unrestrained by any worldly authority whatsoever) to take a further review of the Public Service and to establish such other alterations and amendments therein as might be deemed expedient."[12]

The newly formed American church thus separated liturgical reform from changes in the government, a principle it has continued to live by since that time. This separation was codified by making the Book of Common Prayer a part of the Constitution of the Episcopal Church in the United States. This means that any change in the prayer book is a change to the basic structure of the church, so any revision of the prayer book must be approved by two consecutive sessions of our General Convention.

Though its printing was greeted with both enthusiasm and repudiation, on the whole the 1789 Book of Common Prayer was accepted with relatively little resistance. Like the prayer book of 1549, it seems to have been perceived as "a very godly order . . . agreeable to the Word of God and the primitive Church, very comfortable to all people desiring to live in Christian conversation, and most profitable to the estate of this realm."[13] It provided the foundation for worship in American Episcopal churches for over one hundred years, until it was revised in 1892 and again in 1928, and was the basis for a number of revisions in other churches of the Anglican Communion as well. The liturgical historian Marion Hatchett concludes:

> The judgment of the Episcopal Church, of Anglicanism, and of other communions seems to be that the first American revisers did a better job than they could have guessed in holding fast to what was of value in the old and in winnowing out the chaff from the wheat among the proposals which were before them.[14]

THE 1979 BOOK OF COMMON PRAYER

Even while the Convention of 1928 was approving its revision of the prayer book, it realized that further revision was inevitable. It established "a continuing Liturgical Commission" that would continue to study the prayer book and make suggestions for revisions in light of the changing needs of the church. This commission was largely responsible for the revisions of the 1979 prayer book and is still at work today.

After World War II, the liturgical scholars and theologians of the reconstituted Standing Liturgical Commission began to prepare the way for a revision of the 1928 Book of Common Prayer. Several issues were of concern. As has often been the case with revisions of the prayer book, first was the question of language. Cranmer and the English reformers had written the book "in the language of the people," but that sixteenth-century English was still being used in twentieth-century Episcopal churches. Many people were interested in creating liturgical texts in contemporary American English.

In addition, the discovery of a number of ancient liturgical and scriptural texts in the twentieth century shed new light on the worship of the early church, and it was clear that the Eucharist needed more emphasis than the older prayer books had given it. Many also felt that the theology of the prayer book was overly focused on penitence and sin, and sought to shift the emphasis to the loving forgiveness of God, with a less negative view of humankind.

As the liturgical work of the Standing Liturgical Commission continued, many other Christian denominations were also revising their worship and theology. In the 1960s the Roman Catholic Church shocked the Christian world with its Vatican II *aggiornamento* ("opening the windows"). Among the many new initiatives proposed by this extraordinary council was changing the language of liturgy from Latin to the common language of each nation and culture. Consequently, the impetus for the Episcopal Church to make a similar change in language was strengthened.

Vatican II also led to the formation of a group called the International Consultation on English Texts (ICET), which began looking at many of the traditional liturgical prayers and forms to see if a consensus on a common wording could be found that all Christians could use. These conversations resulted in the development of common translations of the *Kyrie, Gloria, Sanctus, Agnus Dei,* the creeds, and the Lord's Prayer, many of the canticles of the Daily

Office, and other common liturgical texts—all in contemporary English. This group also proposed a new series of readings for Sundays and Holy Days in the church year, one that would offer a larger portion of the Bible to those who regularly attend worship. This common lectionary was a three-year cycle of readings (replacing a one-year cycle in most churches), and included Old Testament readings and portions of Psalms, as well as New Testament and gospel readings.

In the late 1960s a series of trial liturgies were proposed for use in the Episcopal Church so that contemporary texts could be "tested" in the real worship of Episcopalians in their churches. Three separate forms were tried over a nine-year period (*The Liturgy of the Lord's Supper*, and two books known familiarly by the color of their covers as the "green" book and the "zebra" book). Comments and suggestions were solicited from the people and clergy of congregations using the books. The result was the *Draft Proposed Book of Common Prayer*, which first appeared at the General Convention of 1976 (a convention that also authorized the ordination of women to the priesthood and episcopate).

As this General Convention gathered, a controversy had already begun over changing the long—and for many, beloved—tradition of using Elizabethan English (including the formal sentence structures and archaic words, such as "thee" and "doth") as the language of the prayer book. This conflict was dividing the church nearly in half. During the convention the proposed book was revised to include not only the originally proposed contemporary services, but also optional "traditional language" liturgies for the major services of the church: Morning and Evening Prayer, the Holy Eucharist, and the Burial of the Dead. This compromise was approved and the proposed book issued to the church. Its final approval came at the next General Convention in 1979.

The 1979 prayer book has several distinctions. First, of course, is its language. Although other Anglican Provinces (such as Canada, New Zealand, South Africa, and Australia) have also revised their prayer books in the late twentieth century, the American book was the first revision in non-Elizabethan English. However, while language was the most controversial aspect of this revision, many other significant changes were made. The Eucharist was defined as "the principal act of Christian worship on the Lord's Day," thus replacing Sunday Morning Prayer in many parishes. The common translations of the International Consultation on English Texts were incorporated into Episcopal liturgies, and their lectionary for Sundays and Holy Days was adopted, thus insuring a commonality of worship Sunday by Sunday among all the liturgical churches.

In addition, in the 1979 prayer book the service of baptism was redesigned to make the public "covenant" nature of our relationship with God clearer and to spell out what it means to be a follower of Christ. Special liturgies for Lent and Holy Week recovered from the practices of the early and medieval church were included. And confirmation was expanded to include an opportunity for the reaffirmation of baptismal vows and for the reception of individuals from other Christian communions.

Finally, the rubrics (the italicized words that give instructions about what must be or may be done, and who is to do it) were rewritten to be more expansive and inclusive. One of the shortcomings of the 1928 prayer book was its rigid rubrics, which only enhanced the bickering between the "high church" Episcopalians who preferred more elaborate, Catholic-style ritual and the "low church" Episcopalians who worshiped more simply. The loosening of these rubrics made the book much more useful to the whole church, and helped to move the "high-low" conflict to the background of the church's life.

THE LANGUAGE OF THE PRAYER BOOK

The question of language is at the very heart of the prayer book: it is a collection of *words*, after all, and the words with which we speak to one another and to God profoundly affect what we believe to be true about ourselves and God. Our praying shapes our believing: the words we use *matter*. In his volume on the prayer book in the New Church's Teaching Series, Jeffrey Lee notes:

It is important for worshiping communities to know thoroughly the tradition of their prayer. Not for the sake of liturgical correctness, but for the sake of the gospel. To know the classic shape of a eucharistic prayer is not important because it is an interesting piece of historical detail. It is important because it expresses the relationship of the church to the living mystery of the Triune God.[15]

The words we use to describe God—father, mother, friend, unmoved mover, first principle—both express and shape our theology of who God is and how God relates to the creation. Words have power. We all know the damaging effect a continual barrage of negative words can have on our children (as well as on the adults who speak them). If you have traveled to other countries or attended a lecture or church service offered in a language you do not know, you know how isolating and exclusionary language can be. And in an age in which religious language is often used to incite terrorist violence and intolerance of others, we are acutely aware that the words of our prayer can even be a matter of life and death.

Language can be both a window into a deep connection with God and also an impediment to such a relationship. One of the graces of the regular and repeated words of prayer book liturgy is that the words become ingrained in our hearts and minds and no longer need to be "read" but can be prayed in a deeper way that leads beyond words to a connection with God. Like a simple mantra, these fixed and repeated words can open our hearts and minds to deep reverence and love, which is the purpose of Christian worship.

On the other hand, we can also become so attached to the words themselves that we lose sight of the relationship the words were intended to express and encourage. We can become "stuck" in our spiritual lives, praying only with the words and forms that are used in public worship, even in our private devotions. The beautiful words of the prayer book, rather than being windows into God's presence, can become a substitute for a relationship with the living God, keeping God at a safe distance while blocking any real encounter that might change our lives or our understanding of who God is.

In their work of revising the prayer book over the centuries, Anglicans throughout the world continue to work through the ways in which language affects individuals and communities. This is a vital though difficult task because, as we noted before, our praying shapes our believing. The words with which we pray both reflect and affect what we believe to be true about God and ourselves. Attending to the language of our prayer is necessary for keeping our liturgies alive and relevant to the actual lives we live, as well as for ensuring that our common worship is a true and trustworthy source of revelation.

To that end, the language of prayer among Christians has changed dramatically over time, especially in the last half century. Most Episcopal congregations are moving away from the Elizabethan English of the Rite One liturgies of the 1979 prayer book to the contemporary version of American English used in Rite Two. In addition, a number of supplemental prayers and liturgies using "expansive" or "inclusive" language have also appeared in recent years. *Enriching Our Worship 1* and *Enriching Our Worship 2* are two such collections of texts authorized by our General Convention for use in parishes. These supplemental prayers and canticles are adapted from other contemporary Anglican prayer books, from Orthodox and medieval western liturgies, and of course from Scripture. The first volume contains alternative versions of Morning and Evening Prayer, the Great Litany, and the Holy Eucharist; the second includes texts for ministry with those who are sick or dying and for the burial of a child. These prayers and liturgical texts do seek to address such current concerns as the gendered or hierarchical language we use for God, but they also attempt to return "to the resonant imagery of earlier periods in the Church's history," including often neglected writings of the early church and the medieval mystics.[16]

Supplemental texts such as *Enriching Our Worship* are at the heart of ongoing revision of the prayer book. They are, as Presiding Bishop Frank T. Griswold has noted, "part of an ongoing process of listening to what the Spirit is saying to the Church through the diverse experience of those who gather to worship and to celebrate the sacramental rites which fashion and identify us as the People of God."[17] Congregations who use these prayers and liturgies are urged to speak of their experience to members of the Standing Commission on Liturgy and Music as an essential part of the evaluation and discernment process. In that process some prayers will be discarded, others adapted, some committed to memory. The priest and liturgist Jennifer Phillips describes this process of trial use well:

Ultimately, those liturgical texts that will survive over decades, generations, and occasionally centuries of use are those which touch the hearts and minds of many congregations across differences of place and time, bringing together something universal and something particular, something old and something new. Successful texts are those which are cherished. In times of stress and distress, they contain the phrases which spring to the lips for comfort and strength. In times of joy, their words leap to mind as fitting praise for the God who is good beyond all our describing.[18]

The Future of the Prayer Book

On my family's bookshelves we have a collection of well-worn prayer books from our parents and grandparents. Most are bound in leather and are quite small, of a size for devotional use. When I was confirmed in 1979 and again at my ordination in 1987, I was given beautifully bound volumes of the Book of Common Prayer. When my first son was baptized in 1998, his godparents likewise gave him a small leather-bound prayer book, for him to keep for life and pass on to his children. Throughout most of my years as an Episcopalian, I have simply taken the presence of the prayer book in the pew for granted.

And yet in recent years we have seen a subtle but profound movement taking place in the Episcopal Church. As we have lived with the 1979 revision over the years, the focus of our worship has gradually shifted from private devotion to corporate participation. The availability of electronic versions of the Book of Common Prayer has encouraged many parishes to print the entire service in their bulletins, making it easier for people to participate and for worship leaders to adapt the services for a particular event or community. It is thus quite possible now for Episcopalians to be faithful in worship week after week and yet never open a prayer book. As Jeffrey Lee rather starkly notes in *Opening the Prayer Book*, "The prayer book as we have it today may be the last one of its kind."[19] In the future, with the help of technology, we may have a prayer book on CD-ROM or the Internet that is a more expansive collection of liturgies than could ever be bound into a single volume.

This is not to say that the Book of Common Prayer will simply be abandoned in the coming years, however, or will become so expansive as to be unboundaried chaos. Rather, we are coming to a deeper appreciation of what prayer book worship is and can be. We may no longer follow the words of the service in our own devotional-sized leather prayer books as we worship, but we are praying common liturgies that expand our awareness of God in the world. We are now free to look up and around, focusing on the altar and the people who have gathered, aware that we worship as part of a specific Christian community that is in turn part of the church universal. And we worship according to the prayer book tradition, with its gift of "ordered freedom," as Lee puts it.[20] This ability to change and adapt without losing sight of the fundamental, traditional pattern of Christian worship offers Anglicans tremendous latitude to reform their liturgies according to the needs and cultural demands of the time, without disintegrating into a number of individual churches focused simply on their own self-interests, disconnected from the wider community.

As prayer books around the world are revised—sometimes quite radically—to incorporate and reflect the language and culture of the people who use them, the words of Anglican worship have become abundantly multicultural and diverse. And yet the pattern of Anglican worship remains the common ground in which we are rooted. We may no longer hear exactly the same words spoken when we travel to other Episcopal and Anglican churches around the world, but we are still united in the pattern of our common actions. We gather to be reconciled and to pray for one another, the world, and ourselves. We gather to be washed in the waters of baptism and to share in the eucharistic meal that nurtures our common life. We gather to praise and adore the God who creates, loves, redeems, and sustains all that is. Whether we read the words undergirding these actions in a well-worn leather-bound book or follow them in a weekly service bulletin with texts downloaded from the Internet, we are participating in the mystery of worship according to the "ordered freedom" the prayer book tradition both preserves and encourages us to explore.

QUESTIONS FOR REFLECTION AND DISCUSSION

1. What has been your experience of the Book of Common Prayer in your life? Is the prayer book entirely new to you? Do you own and use a prayer book at home? What revision is it?

2. Locate a 1979 prayer book and turn to the table of contents. Do you recognize services you have attended in an Episcopal Church? What words or services are unfamiliar to you? What sections or services would you like to learn more about? Turn to one or two of them and read through them.

3. Again in the 1979 prayer book, read the Preface included from the 1789 prayer book (BCP 9–11). What insights into the process of revising liturgical prayer do you glean from it? What in the Preface surprises you? Confuses you? Is particularly meaningful to you?

Becoming Christian
Holy Baptism

We receive you into the household of God. Confess the faith of Christ crucified, proclaim his resurrection, and share with us in his eternal priesthood.

(BCP 308)

The warm water gently ebbs and flows over the baby's soft skin, her legs and arms slowing their jerky movements, her tiny body relaxing into the familiar watery warmth. Looking at her with loving amazement, her father carefully pours water over her head, gently washing away the residue of her arduous journey. When she is clean he dries her body carefully, and rubs soothing oil into her incredibly soft skin. It is her first bath, her first birth.

Months—perhaps years—later, she is again held by loving arms, surrounded by the familiar faces of her family and friends. They are standing among a crowd of people, gathered around a large stone bowl filled with water. A priest dressed in a long white robe calls out in a strong voice, "Name this child." Her parents and godparents respond with the name they have given her, and she is handed over to the priest, who gathers her in his arms and gently leans her head over the bowl. "I baptize you in the Name of the Father, and of the Son, and of the Holy Spirit," she hears, as warm water is poured over her head three times. The priest carefully dries her head and anoints her forehead with oil in the shape of a cross. As he holds her up high for all to see, she is surprised and delighted to hear welcoming applause and see smiles and joyful tears on so many faces. It is her baptismal bath, her second birth.

Baptism is the sacrament of Christian initiation, the beginning of the Christian life. It has thus traditionally been known as the doorway to all the other sacraments, since it is through baptism that we become members of the church and begin to share in the sacramental life of grace. Yet many of us were baptized as infants and have no memory of the event, so it is not always easy for us to understand the significance of our baptism. Sometimes we learn more of its meaning in hindsight, by participating in the baptismal services of other people in the congregation. Often we come to understand the significance of our baptism more fully later in life. Perhaps over the years we drifted away from the church and are returning now as adults, curiously drawn to rediscover the meaning of the vows made on our behalf long ago. Or perhaps the church has remained a central part of our lives since our baptism, but we feel a need to reevaluate the way we are living our baptismal vows and to discover deeper meanings and more mature expressions of the Christian faith in our lives today. Those of us who were not baptized as children come to receive the sacrament as adults, ready and able to confess the Christian faith for ourselves and enter into new life in Christ.

THE MEANING OF BAPTISM

Water is essential for human survival, and thus is an integral part of our everyday lives. Water quenches our thirst and washes away our grime, and most religious traditions have incorporated some form of the powerful symbolism of water's ability to refresh and cleanse into their liturgical rites. The origins for the Christian water rite—called baptism from the Greek *baptizein*, to dip—can be seen in the Jewish traditions practiced at the time of Jesus. One such tradition was the baptism for Gentile converts to Judaism. In this ritual cleansing from the impurities of the Gentile world, a convert would embrace the Jewish faith, as well as the purity laws ritual practices of Judaism. Another Jewish tradition understood the power of a water rite to cleanse from sin: the baptism of John the

Baptist, for example, emphasized the need for repentance and conversion, forgiveness and a turning away from sin within the Jewish community itself.

Jesus further developed the Jewish understanding of baptism. His own baptism by John in the river Jordan was seen as a fulfillment of John's promise of the coming Messiah, who would baptize "with the Holy Spirit." Jesus later spoke of his death as a kind of baptism: "Are you able to drink the cup that I drink, or be baptized with the baptism that I am baptized with?" (Mark 10:38). Thus in the early church, baptism came to be understood as a kind of death, as dying to sin and rising to new life in Christ. Following the example of Jesus, converts to the faith were "drowned" in deep pools of water and "raised again" to new life in the Spirit. This new life is described by Luke in the book of Acts, when those who were baptized "devoted themselves to the apostles' teaching and fellowship, to the breaking of bread and the prayers" (Acts 2:42). The prayer book echoes these words in the promises we make in the Baptismal Covenant (BCP 304).

In the Episcopal Church we have softened the dying and rising imagery of the sacrament by baptizing infants with a few sprinkles of water, but the powerful symbolism of cleansing and rebirth remains. I confess that in my own garbled religious history I have been baptized twice, both times as a teenager: first neatly sprinkled in a Presbyterian church, then later immersed in a lake with other fervent charismatic believers on retreat. Both were equally significant events in my life at the time, yet it has only been in the years since, as I have participated in the baptismal services of other new Christians, that my understanding of the meaning of my baptism has grown and deepened.

On a much larger scale, the church's theology of baptism has likewise changed over time. Many Christians in the early church believed that sins committed after baptism could not be forgiven, so baptism was delayed until old age unless death seemed imminent. Over time the church came to understand that God's forgiveness is more generous, and that sins could be forgiven at any time, before or after baptism. Concern over high infant mortality rates encouraged parents to baptize their children as soon as possible after birth, especially when baptism was understood primarily in terms of forgiveness of sins and parents worried over the eternal fate of an unbaptized infant. Again, today we understand baptism not as an "insurance policy" for babies whose untimely death would place them in the hands of an angry God of judgment, but as a sign of their participation in the family of a welcoming God whose Son loved the children gathered around him.

For infants as well as adults, we are recovering an earlier association of baptism with membership in the church, especially since the adoption of the 1979 Book of Common Prayer. Although the forgiveness of sins is still an essential part of our understanding of the meaning of this sacrament of initiation, the focus is more on the incorporation of a new member into the community. It is through participation in the life of the church, no matter what our age, that we come to understand what it means to be a Christian. Charles Price and Louis Weil describe this participation well:

> Baptized children are eligible for all the benefits of belonging to the kingdom of God—love, joy, peace, forgiveness. They are responsible for whatever Christian obligations they are able to undertake, more and more as they mature. Children *grow* into the meaning of their membership in the people of God, but they belong to the community all along.[21]

For this reason in many Episcopal churches today infants and young children will begin to receive communion as soon as they are baptized, and they are welcomed to all the sacraments as they are able and have need of them. Their intellectual understanding of the sacrament will grow with time, but is not a prerequisite for receiving God's grace.

BAPTISM IN THE EARLY CHURCH

Documents from the early church reveal that the way baptisms were celebrated in the centuries immediately following the life and death of Jesus varied from place to place, though there were common threads among them. All used water in some form, either in a large pool of fresh, running (sometimes called "living") water, or in a basin or bowl. And all incorporated prayer and words of baptism in the name of the triune God—the Father, Son, and Holy Spirit.

As early as the Day of Pentecost, fifty days after Jesus' resurrection, the followers of Jesus viewed baptism as one of the means by which salvation and the gift of the Holy Spirit were given. After Peter's passionate sermon on that momentous day, those who were present "were cut to the heart" and asked the apostles what they should do.

Peter said to them, "Repent, and be baptized every one of you in the name of Jesus Christ so that your sins may be forgiven; and you will receive the gift of the Holy Spirit." (Acts 2:38)

Apparently baptism in the name of the Trinity was already being practiced within the community in which the evangelist Matthew was writing during the last third of the first century:

> And Jesus came and said to them, "All authority in heaven and on earth has been given to me. Go therefore and make disciples of all nations, baptizing them in the name of the Father and of the Son and of the Holy Spirit, and teaching them to obey everything that I have commanded you." (Matthew 28:18–20)

In a second-century account by Justin Martyr we are given another glimpse of how baptisms were performed in the early church. In this passage we see the importance of baptism not just as a sign of salvation and the forgiveness of sins, but also as a means of "rebirth" as a member of the Christian community:

> As many as are persuaded and believe that these things which we teach and describe are true, and undertake to live accordingly, are taught to pray and ask God, while fasting, for the forgiveness of sins; and we pray and fast with them. Then they are led to a place where there is water, and they are reborn after the manner of rebirth by which we also were reborn: for they are then washed in the water in the name of the Father and Lord God of all things, and of our Saviour Jesus Christ, and of the Holy Spirit.[22]

By the beginning of the third century, at least in some places, the church had developed a process called the catechumenate for new converts. Those who wished to become Christians sought sponsors who could vouch for their sincerity and present them to the church for instruction. The newcomers were admitted to a three-year period of preparation that included study, prayer, and the practice of good works. After that time, several weeks before Easter they became candidates and entered into an intensive period of preparation and instruction in the gospel.

Candidates spent the Thursday, Friday, and Saturday before the Easter Vigil in prayer and fasting, as they continued their instruction in the Christian faith. They were then baptized during the vigil, often at dawn. According to the *Apostolic Tradition* (written around 215, probably in Rome), after the candidates renounced "Satan, all his servants, and all his works," the presbyter (we call them priests today) anointed the candidate's whole body with the oil of exorcism, just as the Romans would anoint themselves with oil before entering the baths. The deacon would then take the candidate into the water, which was to be cold and flowing. After the candidate was asked to confess his or her belief in "God, the Father almighty," the presbyter pushed the candidate down into the water. This was followed by another question:

> Do you believe in Jesus Christ, the Son of God, who was born of the Holy Spirit from the Virgin Mary, and was crucified under Pontius Pilate, and was dead and buried, and rose again the third day, alive from the dead, and ascended into heaven, and sat at the right hand of the Father, and will come to judge the living and the dead?

After the candidate replied, "I believe," he or she was immersed again. Finally, the presbyter asked a third question that was followed by a third immersion: "Do you believe in the Holy Spirit, and the holy church, and the resurrection of the flesh?" If the words of these ancient questions sound familiar to you, it is with good reason: the creeds we say today in our liturgies, especially the

Apostles' Creed and the Nicene Creed, grew and developed from baptismal forms such as this.[23]

After the confession of faith and triple immersion, in some places the newly baptized person was fully anointed again, this time with the oil of thanksgiving, or chrism, just as a newborn would be anointed after a first bath or a king or queen would be anointed when taking the crown. Anointing has long been associated with kingship, and the early church anointed converts with oil just as Jesus was "anointed" by the Holy Spirit as the Messiah at his baptism. In the Judaism of Jesus' time, converts were "branded" with the *Taw* (T), the last letter of the Hebrew alphabet, to signify the name of God and his "ownership" of the newly baptized Jew. In much the same way, in the early church the newly baptized were marked on the forehead with the sign of the cross. Dom Gregory Dix explains that this use of chrism (or blessed oil) "signifies the cleansing of the bath, the anointing of kings and priests, the 'seal' of baptism, and incorporation into Christ, which title means 'The Anointed One.' The word 'christen' derived from the chrism: to be 'christened' is to be 'anointed.'"[24]

After the anointing with oil, the new Christian was then clothed in a white robe and taken into the church to exchange the peace and participate in the Eucharist for the first time. The liturgical scholar Marion Hatchett describes the impact of these early baptismal rites:

> The experience of initiation was so traumatic that those who experienced it felt that they had died and been raised, that they had been reborn, that the ones with whom they now had most in common were those who had undergone the same initiation. An old baptistry inscription reads: "Nothing can separate those who are reborn. They are one: one baptism, one Spirit, one faith, one God and Father."[25]

Many of us have undergone initiation rites other than baptism, perhaps to a fraternity or sorority, a club, military unit, or school, and these sometimes traumatic rites have changed and marked us much as baptism did the baptismal candidates in the early church.

BAPTISM AT THE REFORMATION

Over time, of course, the rituals and meaning of baptism adapted to the changing circumstances of church and society. In the early church, Christians were a small persecuted sect. Prospective believers were carefully screened, for spies and false converts could cost the lives of an entire community. Intensive preparation for baptism often continued for at least three years, and only after their baptism were converts initiated into the "mysteries" of the faith by sharing in the Holy Eucharist. The end of persecution and the establishment of Christendom required less rigorous screening of candidates, and encouraged even those whose faith was less certain or vigorous to consider themselves Christian. The faces of new converts grew increasingly younger and the length of preparation shorter until, by the time of Charlemagne in the eighth century, infant baptism within eight days of birth had become the norm.

As the doctrine of original sin developed in the early Middle Ages, candidates were baptized at younger ages, and this increased frequency of infant baptism led to a remarkably shortened period of preparation. Practices varied widely concerning when and how the anointing with oil was done—or whether it was done at all. The significance of the sacrament of baptism declined in the Middle Ages: no longer a public ceremony of initiation and commitment at the heart of the foundational liturgy of the church, the Easter Vigil, infant baptisms were increasingly done quietly in brief, private ceremonies in the afternoon, with only the parents and godparents present.

Many of the reformers sought to restore the sacrament of baptism as a meaningful rite of rebirth. Some Reformation churches, such as the Anabaptists, rejected infant baptism and rebaptized by immersion those who had been baptized as infants. Martin Luther's churches in Germany insisted that baptisms take place in the context of the Sunday Eucharist, not in private ceremonies. Likewise, the 1549 Book of Common Prayer considered baptism a public rite, noting that it "should not be ministered but upon Sundays and other holy days, when the most number of people may come together."[26]

This movement of baptism from the liturgical sidelines into the midst of the gathered community is significant, for it is only when baptism is a public sacrament that the entire church can be given the opportunity—and responsibility—to welcome the newly baptized. And, as we noted above, participating in the baptisms of others is an important way for us to deepen our understanding of the meaning of our own baptism into Christ's one, holy, catholic church, as we reaffirm our faith and recognize ourselves in the sometimes very different faces of the newly baptized.

BAPTISM IN THE EPISCOPAL CHURCH TODAY

In the Episcopal Church today we are the inheritors of many baptismal traditions, and our baptismal liturgies attempt to incorporate these practices while affirming the early church's experience of baptism as a rite of real transformation and power. Perhaps the first encounter many people have of this renewed emphasis on baptism is when parents ask to schedule their infant's baptism.

Although every congregation makes its own decisions concerning the Sundays on which it will celebrate baptisms, the 1979 Book of Common Prayer makes the connection between baptism and the feasts of the church year clear by recommending that baptisms be reserved for the four traditional feast days with baptismal connections: the Easter Vigil; the Day of Pentecost; the first Sunday after the Epiphany, which is the day we celebrate Jesus' baptism; and All Saints' Day. The Sunday on which the bishop visits a congregation is also considered an appropriate day for baptisms, as the bishop's visit signifies the unity of the one church. If for pastoral reasons baptisms cannot be limited to these principal feast days, then the prayer book allows that they may be celebrated on other occasions, but the sacrament should be "administered within the Eucharist as the chief service on a Sunday or other feast" (BCP 298).

The length and content of the preparation for baptism varies considerably among Episcopal churches. In some places you will find the restored catechumenate, with liturgical rites and study emphasizing the process of formation in the Christian faith prior to the sacrament of initiation. In other places, infant candidates and their parents simply arrive at the church on Sunday morning for a brief introduction to the service before the baptism—it is assumed that formation in faith will take place afterward, as the newly baptized are incorporated as members of the community. And most Episcopal churches fall somewhere in between, adapting the length and content of preparation to the needs of each candidate.

THE BAPTISMAL LITURGY

Since baptisms today normally take place in the context of the Sunday Eucharist, and often on a feast day, when you arrive the church will be adorned in the liturgical colors of that season or feast. The candidates for baptism, along with their sponsors, will usually be asked to sit together in a convenient place near the font, which may be at the back of the church, signifying baptism as the entrance or doorway into the church. The service begins with the usual opening sentences, but then immediately focuses our attention on the unity to which baptism witnesses:

> *Celebrant* There is one Body and one Spirit;
> *People* There is one hope in God's call to us;
> *Celebrant* One Lord, one Faith, one Baptism;
> *People* One God and Father of all. (BCP 299)

After hearing the lessons from Scripture and the sermon, the celebrant asks the sponsors to present their candidates for baptism. The sponsors for infants and children usually include their parents as well as their godparents, and the sponsors are asked two questions:

> Will you be responsible for seeing that the child you present is brought up in the Christian faith and life?

> Will you by your prayers and witness help this child to grow into the full stature of Christ? (BCP 302)

The sponsors thus promise not only to attend to the formation in faith of the child, but also to remain faithful to their own life of prayer and witness.

A series of questions then follows, asked either of the sponsors on behalf of an infant, or of the candidates themselves. The questions follow an ancient tradition in the Eastern churches of Jerusalem and

Antioch: three renunciations of evil followed by three affirmations of faith in Jesus Christ. In some places in the fourth century, candidates faced west for the renunciations (as a sign of rejection) and turned toward the east (signifying light and life) for the affirmations, "symbolizing their inward and spiritual conversion by their visible turning."[27]

At this point the baptismal service clearly becomes a sacrament of the Christian community and not a private ceremony, as the celebrant asks the congregation this question:

> Will you who witness these vows do all in your power to support these persons in their life in Christ? (BCP 303)

When the congregation knows the candidates and is willing and able to respond with a resounding "We will," it can be a moment of significant transformation for candidates and congregation alike, affirming that we are not alone in our Christian journey. In making and receiving the promise of the community's support in the years to come, we recognize that baptism is an initiation into the common life of the church as the one Body of Christ.

Likewise, the entire community—not just the candidates—affirms the Baptismal Covenant. You may recognize in this covenant the words of the Apostles' Creed. That is because the origins of this creed lie in ancient baptismal formulas repeated as the candidates were asked "Do you believe. . . ?" and then immersed in water three times. The creed is followed by five questions about our intention to grow and mature in the Christian faith. We promise to continue to learn from Scripture and the church's teaching and to be nourished by the Eucharist and prayer. We promise to resist evil and to "repent and return to the Lord" when we fail. And we promise to proclaim the gospel in our words and actions, to serve others in love, and to "strive for justice and peace among all people" (BCP 304–5).

After the congregation prays for the candidates, we come to the heart of the baptismal service. Over the baptismal water, the celebrant offers a prayer of thanksgiving that echoes the structure of our eucharistic prayer of thanksgiving. We thank God for the gift of water and for our redemption in Jesus Christ. Then we affirm our belief in the meaning of baptism "in the Name of the Father, and of the Son, and of the Holy Spirit." Finally, we ask the Holy Spirit to sanctify the waters of baptism "that those who here are cleansed from sin and born again may continue for ever in the risen life of Jesus Christ our Savior" (BCP 306–7).

Then the sponsors present the candidates by name and the celebrant either immerses them in water or pours water on their heads, repeating the ancient formula in the name of the Trinity, based on Jesus' words at the end of Matthew's gospel. After the newly baptized are dried with a towel, the celebrant prays that God will sustain them and "give them an inquiring and discerning heart, the courage to will and to persevere, a spirit to know and to love you, and the gift of joy and wonder in all your works" (BCP 308).

Following the prayer the celebrant anoints the new Christians with the oil of chrism, usually in the form of the sign of the cross marked on the forehead. Although the meaning and practice of anointing in the baptismal liturgy has varied over the centuries, in most places some form of anointing has been included in the rite. In the early church the sign of anointing with oil was so significant that one writer could say, "We are called Christians because we are anointed with the chrism of God."[28]

In some congregations new Christians are given a small candle lit from the flame of the paschal candle (see BCP 313). This ancient custom, beloved in many congregations, is a symbol of our participation in the light of Christ. In my family we light our children's baptismal candles during a brief celebration of prayer and feasting every year on the anniversary of their baptism.

Finally, the newly baptized and anointed Christians are formally welcomed into the church community with words that never fail to make us aware of the glorious weight of our call as the Body of Christ in the world:

We receive you into the household of God. Confess the faith of Christ crucified, proclaim his resurrection, and share with us in his eternal priesthood. (BCP 308)

The congregation welcomes them warmly into the fellowship of the church in the exchange of the peace. In some parishes, those who are newly baptized, with infants held by the priest or godparents, walk in procession around the church during the peace so everyone can greet them.

After the exchange of the peace, the service continues as usual with the Holy Eucharist, and the newly baptized receive communion, perhaps for the first time. In the early church catechumens were not permitted to attend the Eucharist or receive communion until after their baptism, and although this practice is no longer universal in the Episcopal Church, for many their first communion as baptized Christians is a memorable moment in their life in Christ.

The alternative concluding prayer for the baptismal liturgy expresses well the significance of baptism as a loving and transforming bond that is "indissoluble" because it is established by God (BCP 298):

> All praise and thanks to you, most merciful Father, for adopting us as your own children, for incorporating us into your holy Church, and for making us worthy to share in the inheritance of the saints in light. (BCP 311)

In our dying and rising in the waters of baptism, we are adopted as children of God and we enter into the fellowship of Christ's body in heaven and on earth. Our life in that community of the church is sustained by prayer and study, and especially by our sharing in the bread and wine of the Lord's Supper. And so it is to the Eucharist that we turn now.

QUESTIONS FOR REFLECTION AND DISCUSSION

1. If you have been baptized, what was your experience of that sacrament? Were you an infant? Child? Teenager? Adult? What memories do you have of the event, or what stories have you been told by those who were there? What significance does your baptism hold for you today?

2. What initiatory rites have you undergone in your life? What significance did they have for you at the time? How have they changed your life today?

3. Have you participated in the baptism of another person? What was your role? How did your participation in the sacrament affect your understanding of your own baptism or life of faith?

Sharing a Common Meal
The Holy Eucharist

We celebrate the memorial of our redemption, O Father, in this sacrifice of praise and thanksgiving. Recalling his death, resurrection, and ascension, we offer you these gifts. Sanctify them by your Holy Spirit to be for your people the Body and Blood of your Son, the holy food and drink of new and unending life in him.

(BCP 363)

The elderly woman opens the china cupboard and carefully takes out her mother's dinner plates. As she places each one on the large table with its freshly ironed white linen tablecloth, she remembers all the meals that have been shared on these dishes. So many Thanksgiving dinners, birthday parties, and Christmas celebrations, the room ringing with laughter, animated conversation, and the voices of children. The subdued yet loving gathering after father's funeral, and then her mother's. So many prayers of gratitude for God's gracious generosity offered before those meals.

She thinks of all the people who have been nourished by the food from these plates: her parents, children, brothers, sisters, grandchildren, friends. Some of the plates are chipped from their years of use. What memories they hold; what stories they could tell! Each year they are a silent witness to the passing of time, as the people who eat from them grow and change, laugh and argue, celebrate and mourn.

And then one day those who shared the meals no longer come to the table, but they are never forgotten. They remain in memory, part of the family whose very identity was shaped and strengthened year after year by this breaking of bread at the family table.

The priest walks softly to the altar in the empty, half-lit church, making sure everything is ready for the service. As they have every Sunday for as many years as the priest can remember, the altar guild has carefully arranged the silver chalice and paten on the freshly ironed white linen cloth. Everything is in its place. The priest notices a few dents in the beautifully polished silver, the result of many years of frequent use. As she looks out at the empty pews that will soon be filled with parishioners and guests, she thinks of how many hands have reached out for the bread of communion around this table, seeking comfort and strength in the midst of troubles, offering thanks for abundant blessings. She remembers all those who have gone before and imagines what this church will be like for those who will come after. It is here, at the altar, that Christians have gathered week by week to reaffirm their identity as followers of Christ, to share in the Lord's Supper and thus be nourished for their ministries of service in world.

THE ORIGINS OF THE EUCHARIST

If you attend a Sunday service in the Episcopal Church today you will most likely find yourself at a service we call the Holy Eucharist. Only a few decades ago you might have encountered a form of Morning Prayer instead, but the 1979 prayer book, with its emphasis on restoring the Sunday Eucharist to its earlier place of weekly priority, has encouraged the celebration of the Holy Eucharist every Sunday and that practice is now well established.

The liturgy of the Eucharist goes by any number of names— Holy Communion, the Lord's Supper, the Mass, the Supper of the Lord—but the heart of the service is hearing the Word of God proclaimed and sharing bread and wine in the context of thanksgiving. Indeed, the word "Eucharist" is Greek for "thanksgiving." The origins of the Christian Eucharist are ancient, rooted in the common Jewish practice of gathering regularly for meals of thanksgiving with prayers, though for Jesus' disciples the meal took on added meaning at the Last Supper they shared with their Lord. These prayers and specific acts of eating were gradually formalized into liturgical rites during the centuries following Jesus' death and resurrection.

In the gospels and Paul's letters we find several accounts of the Last Supper, and although these accounts do not all agree—in Matthew, Mark, and Luke the meal is the Passover supper, while in John it is a supper on the night *before* the Passover—we can see in them the beginnings of the rite we call the Eucharist. According to Mark's gospel, at the Passover supper Jesus celebrated with his twelve disciples on the night before he died, Jesus "took a loaf of bread, and after blessing it he broke it, gave it to them, and said, 'Take; this is my body.'" After they ate the bread he then took a cup of wine, and "after giving thanks he gave it to them, and all of them drank from it. He said to them, 'This is my blood of the covenant, which is poured out for many. Truly I tell you, I will never again drink of the fruit of the vine until that day when I drink it new in the kingdom of God'" (Mark 14:22–25). Clearly in this account there are strong parallels to the Jewish practice of identifying various foods at the Passover supper and attributing symbolic meaning to them.

In John's gospel the Last Supper takes place on the night before the Passover. The eminent liturgical scholar Dom Gregory Dix argues convincingly that the origins of our Eucharist are more likely to be found in the Jewish meal called the *chabûrah* supper that John describes.[29] At the time of Jesus it was common to belong to a *chabûrah*, a small group of friends who gathered regularly for devotion and service. These informal societies existed within the Jewish religious communities much as our small Bible study, prayer, or fellowship groups exist within congregations today. Part of their devotional practice was to share a common meal every week, offering prayers of thanksgiving before the bread, wine, and each food that was served. These formal prayers would have been familiar to all practicing Jews of that time: "Blessed be Thou, O Lord our God, eternal King, Who bringest forth bread from the earth. . . Who createst the fruit of the vine."

In Jesus' Last Supper we see parallels to this practice of giving thanks before each part of the meal, though the symbolism he attributes to the bread and wine on that night would certainly have startled the disciples. Dix concludes that "what our Lord did at the last supper, then, was not to establish any new rite." Rather, he attached to the eating of bread and the drinking of wine—which were "the only two things which He could be sure they would do together regularly"— a new meaning of connection with his impending death.[30]

Whether the specific origins of the Eucharist are in the Passover meal or the Jewish *chabûrah* suppers—or both—it is clear that the first Christians continued to gather for weekly meals after the crucifixion. At these suppers they gave thanks for all creation, including bread and wine, and for the redemption of God's people through Christ. But the prayers were also now imbued with a symbolic connection to the death and resurrection of their Lord as they awaited his imminent return. As they shared in the breaking of bread and drank from the cup, they knew the risen Jesus was once again present in their midst.

THE EUCHARIST IN THE EARLY CHURCH

We are fortunate today to benefit from the twentieth-century discoveries of a number of very early liturgical commentaries and texts, though some are quite fragmentary, and from their incorporation into the rites of our 1979 prayer book. These writings give us a glimpse of the profound connections between what we do on Sunday mornings and what Christians have done on Sunday mornings for centuries upon centuries. Though the "externals" of the eucharistic liturgy have ebbed and flowed over time—adding ceremonies and elaborating prayers here, simplifying the services there, speaking in Latin, in Greek, in English—we might be surprised at how much we would recognize as familiar if we were able to attend a Eucharist with members of the early church.

One of the earliest descriptions we have of the Eucharist was written by Justin Martyr about 150 C.E. He describes a rather simple service to "recall" the redemptive acts of God in Christ Jesus. "On the day named after the sun," the Christians gather to hear "the memoirs of the apostles or the writings of the prophets." Following the readings and homily, the people stand to pray, and bread and wine with water are presented. Then "the president offers prayers of thanksgiving, according to his ability, and the people give their assent with an 'Amen!'" The gifts are then distributed and all who are present share in them, with deacons taking them to the Christians in that community who are absent.[31]

It seems clear from Justin's description that at least by the middle of the second century in some places the eucharistic sharing of bread and wine has been separated from the full meal of the Jewish *chabûrah* suppers. We see the rumblings of the trouble that may have encouraged this split, at least among the Gentile Christian communities, in Paul's First Letter to the Corinthians. He admonishes them for dividing into factions at their common suppers:

> When you come together, it is not really to eat the Lord's supper. For when the time comes to eat, each of you goes ahead with your own supper, and one goes hungry and another becomes drunk. What! Do you not have homes to eat and drink in? Or do you show contempt for the church of God and humiliate those who have nothing? (1 Cor 11:20–22)

Paul's solution is for those who are hungry to eat their meals at home first, and then to come together to share as one in the Lord's Supper (11:33–34). We still follow his advice today.

By the late second and early third centuries, the shape of the Eucharist as we know it was largely established. In the *Apostolic Tradition*, a third-century text compiled by a theologian named Hippolytus, we see almost all of the elements that were passed on through the Middle Ages and into the Anglican prayer books of the Reformation, and thus on to the Episcopal Church today. Hippolytus's eucharistic prayer, for example, begins with this dialogue between the celebrant and the congregation:

> The Lord be with you.
> *And with thy spirit.*
> Lift up your hearts.
> *We lift up unto the Lord.*
> Let us give thanks unto the Lord.
> *It is meet and right.*[32]

We know this exchange well from our experience of the Eucharist each Sunday.

Following the dialogue, Hippolytus's prayer contains three other familiar elements: the thanksgivings and prayers of blessing; the words of institution, often called the memorial or *anamnesis*—a Greek word meaning remembrance; and the invocation of the Holy Spirit, with prayers for the church. The exact words differ from those in our prayer book, of course, but the meaning is the same. See the words of institution in Hippolytus, for example:

> Who, when he was betrayed to his willing death, that he might bring to nought death, and break the bonds of the devil, and tread hell under foot, and give light to the righteous, and set up a boundard post, and manifest his resurrection, taking bread and giving thanks to thee, said: Take, eat; this is my body, which is broken for you. And likewise, also the cup, saying: This is my blood, which is shed for you. As often as ye perform this, perform my memorial.[33]

In one of the eucharistic prayers in the 1979 Book of Common Prayer, we have these words of institution:

> On the night he was handed over to suffering and death, our Lord Jesus Christ took bread; and when he had given thanks to you, he broke it, and gave it to his disciples, and said, "Take, eat: This is my Body, which is given for you. Do this for the remembrance of me." After supper he took the cup of wine; and when he had given thanks, he gave it to them, and said, "Drink this, all of you: This is my Blood of the new Covenant, which is shed for you and for many for the forgiveness of sins. Whenever you drink it, do this for the remembrance of me." (BCP 362–63)

Despite the differences in wording, the meaning and the form of the eucharistic prayer Hippolytus describes has remained intact over the years, adapted and repeated by countless Christians in countless Eucharists throughout the world. The repetition over time and in all places is part of the power of the words, giving us a language to take part in this eternal and ongoing conversation between God and humanity.

THE EUCHARIST AT THE REFORMATION

In the first English prayer book of 1549 the title for the liturgy of the Eucharist is "The Supper of the Lorde and the Holy Communion, commonly called the Masse." In these three ascriptions we see the combination of Reformation, English, and medieval Catholic influences on the service.[34] Although the order of service is different from what we are accustomed to (the service starts with the Lord's Prayer and the exchange of the peace takes place at the end of the eucharistic prayer but before communion, for example), we would readily recognize most of the elements. As early as the 1552 prayer book the order was established that remained largely intact through a number of revisions, including our 1979 book.

Perhaps the most significant change Thomas Cranmer made to the eucharistic liturgy was the restoration of the invocation of the Holy Spirit, an ancient prayer lost over time in the West, asking the Spirit to "bless and sanctify" the "gifts of bread and wine." The Latin rite had no such invocation, but focused rather on the words of institution. Using the text from the Eastern Liturgy of Saint Basil as his foundation, Cranmer inserted the words "with thy Holy Spirit and Word vouchsafe to bless and sanctify these thy gifts of bread and wine" just before the words of institution.[35]

We should not assume that simply because the Eucharist was offered in English every Sunday during these Reformation years, however, all the people shared in that communion. The rubrics for the 1549 prayer book direct that "all must attend weekly, but need communicate but once a year." The rubrics further direct that communion was to be taken "in both kindes," which meant that the people were to be given both bread and wine. In the Middle Ages it had become common for the people to be given bread only, if they were given anything at all, out of overzealous reverence for the consecrated host and fastidiousness over sinful human nature. In such a liturgical culture the symbolism of a meal of thanksgiving shared by followers of Jesus—with the Lord present in their midst—was often so obscured as to be unrecognizable.

One of the definitive struggles of the Reformation was the theology of the Eucharist. Is the Eucharist a memorial service in which we remember with thanksgiving Jesus' acts of redemption (memorialism), or is it a service in which bread and wine are miraculously changed into the body and blood of Christ (transubstantiation)? If Christ is truly present, *how* is he present? In Luke's gospel we hear the story of the disciples going to Emmaus on the first Easter Sunday, as the risen Jesus is "made known to them in the breaking of the bread" (Luke 24:35). The Reformation church struggled mightily and often violently with the question of exactly *how* Christ was made known in that breaking of bread and sharing of wine.

The English church was torn by this question as well, and the divisions are reflected in the prayers and communion rites of the various editions of the Book of Common Prayer. We can still see the evidence of these struggles in our prayer book today. For example, when you receive communion during a service using Rite One in our 1979 Book of Common Prayer, the person distributing the bread will usually say the following words:

The Body of our Lord Jesus Christ, which was given for thee, preserve thy body and soul unto everlasting life. Take and eat this in remembrance that Christ died for thee, and feed on him in thy heart by faith, with thanksgiving. (BCP 338)

The first of these two sentences, with its more traditional reference to Christ's "Body," is from the 1549 prayer book. The second sentence, with its Reformation emphasis on "remembrance," replaced those words in the 1552 book and extremist reformers added an explanation that became known as the "black rubric." Although communicants were required to kneel to receive communion, their kneeling "is not ment thereby, that any adoration is doone, or oughte to bee doone, either unto the Sacramental bread or wyne." The reformers were concerned to remove from the prayer book any hint of the complex doctrine of transubstantiation, which was usually misunderstood to mean that the bread and wine of the Eucharist physically became the body and blood of Christ. They believed this doctrine had led to superstitious and idolatrous forms of worship in the veneration of the bread and wine itself.

These two communion sentences were combined in Elizabeth's effort to produce a more inclusively moderate revision of the prayer book in 1559 (in which the "black rubric" was quietly dropped), and have thus remained together for almost 450 years. They allow for a broad spectrum of beliefs about Christ's presence in the bread and wine of communion, but in characteristically Anglican deference to mystery do not offer a defining theology of the Eucharist. This deference is well embodied in the often quoted statement concerning Holy Communion attributed to Queen Elizabeth I:

> Christ was the Word who spake it,
> Christ took the bread and brake it,
> And what his word doth make it,
> That I believe and take it.

As the former Archbishop of Canterbury Michael Ramsey once summarized, "Trusting that because Christ says so, Christ is truly present, and Christ gives his own self to us as his gift. That was Queen Elizabeth, and that was the Prayer Book she used."[36]

Richard Hooker, a parish priest and foundational Anglican theologian who lived during the reign of Queen Elizabeth, would have concurred:

> Let it therefore be sufficient for me presenting myself at the Lord's table to know what there I receive from him, without searching or inquiring of the manner of how Christ performeth His promise. . . . What these elements are in themselves it skilleth not, it is enough that to me which take them they are the body and blood of Christ.[37]

It is this trust in the real though mysterious and undefined presence of Christ in the Eucharist that continues to characterize much of an Anglican theology of the Eucharist today. We do not need to know *how* Christ is present in the bread and wine in order to know, Sunday after Sunday, that he *is*.

THE EUCHARIST IN THE EPISCOPAL CHURCH TODAY

Unlike its predecessors, the 1979 Book of Common Prayer we use in the Episcopal Church today contains a number of alternative rites for the Holy Eucharist. This variety reflects the work of liturgical scholars and archaeologists in the twentieth century who discovered and translated several important manuscripts dating from the early church, as well as ecumenical movements leading all the liturgical churches to develop modern liturgies based on the same common texts. It also reflects the concern of the prayer book revisers to provide liturgies that encompass the broad spectrum of worship traditions and piety in the Episcopal Church.

We thus have two primary rites in the 1979 prayer book: Rite One retains the Elizabethan English beloved by so many who grew up with the 1928 prayer book, while Rite Two offers the Eucharist in modern language and imagery. Each rite is divided into two basic parts: The Word of God and the Holy Communion. We gather to hear the Word of God in Scripture, to pray together, to make our confession and be restored to the fellowship of the church, and to be nurtured and fed in the sharing of a common meal of bread and wine.

The 1979 Book of Common Prayer also offers An Order for Celebrating the Holy Eucharist, commonly known as Rite Three (BCP 400–405). This simple outline allows for flexibility in both style and content, while maintaining the traditional format and elements of the service that have been part of the church's worship for centuries. Since only the outline of the rite is given, the leaders and participants must supply most of the texts and prayers, though two forms for the eucharistic prayer are provided. Rite Three Eucharists are "not intended for use at the principal Sunday or weekly celebration of the Holy Eucharist" (BCP 400), so you will normally encounter them in situations such as youth group gatherings or parish retreats.

The simple Rite Three order for the Eucharist shows clearly the general shape of the Eucharist as we know it today. We gather, hear and respond to Scripture, pray for the world and the church, greet one another in the Lord's name, prepare the table, offer Eucharist, break the bread, and share in communion. No matter what particular words are spoken or how elaborate or plain the ceremony is, this format is one those who are new to the Episcopal Church will usually recognize and over time become accustomed to. Other generations would have been familiar with somewhat different arrangements of the various elements, but in general through the centuries the eucharistic liturgy has maintained this basic outline of gathering to hear the Word of God and to share in the Holy Communion.

The Word of God

The Entrance Rite

The service begins with some kind of opening greeting or salutation, which changes according to the season of the church year. In Lent, for example, the celebrant begins, "Bless the Lord who forgives all our sins," and we respond, "His mercy endures for ever" (BCP 355). This greeting is usually followed by a prayer known as the collect for purity, which dates back at least to the eleventh century, though it was said privately by the priest until the 1552 prayer book included it in the public order for worship.

Several options follow the collect for purity, depending on the season of the church year and the occasion on which a particular Eucharist is celebrated. A song of praise such as the *Gloria in excelsis*, a hymn from the early church, may be sung on Sunday mornings or feast days. The *Kyrie eleison* ("Lord, have mercy") is often used during Lent and for simple services that do not include music. The *Trisagion* ("Holy God, Holy and Mighty, Holy Immortal One"), like the *Kyrie*, is generally repeated three times, in keeping with ancient custom. The *Trisagion* is a hymn from the Eastern churches that has long been included in liturgies in the West.

A prayer called the collect of the day then follows. Collects are prayers that vary according to the day or occasion. Originally the word "collect" probably signified the "collecting" or summing up of the prayers of all those gathered to pray, though it has also come to mean a prayer with a particular structure: a preamble, a petition, and a conclusion. We can see this structure in the collect for the feast of the Transfiguration, for example:

> [*Preamble*] O God, who on the holy mount revealed to chosen witnesses your well-beloved Son, wonderfully transfigured, in raiment white and glistening: [*Petition*] Mercifully grant that we, being delivered from the disquietude of this world, may by faith behold the King in his beauty; [*Conclusion*] who with you, O Father, and you, O Holy Spirit, lives and reigns, one God, for ever and ever. *Amen.* (BCP 243)

The 1979 prayer book contains collects from a variety of sources and ages, from the early church through the English prayer books to newly composed prayers of the twentieth century. Some collects focus on particular feast days; others incorporate theological themes, such as the Holy Trinity or the Incarnation. A collect is provided in the prayer book for each Sunday in the church year, as well as for the days of Holy Week, Easter Week and major feasts. We also have a variety of collects on topics concerning the Christian life, such as the collects For Vocation in Daily Work, For the Sick, and For Peace (BCP 251–61).

The Lessons

After the collect we come to the primary focus of this first half of the eucharistic liturgy: the proclamation of the Word of God. Christians have gathered to hear the reading and interpretation of the Scriptures since their earliest days. Indeed, in his commentary on the 1979 Book of Common Prayer, Marion Hatchett notes:

> The early Christians met from the first for services which consisted principally of the reading and exposition of the Scriptures. For this they had the precedent of the services in the Jewish synagogue. Readings in the synagogue were either chosen at the reader's discretion or were a part of "in course" readings (*lectio continua*) or were from a fixed lectionary. The early Christians soon added readings from Christian writings to those from the Old Testament; the books of the New Testament were in fact

largely selected from Christian writings which had come into general use in the church's worship.[38]

Over time the church has developed a number of different lectionaries; in the Episcopal Church today we use the Revised Common Lectionary, which is also used by a number of other liturgical denominations.

The number of lessons read in a celebration of the Holy Eucharist varies from one to four or more. A common custom for a Sunday service is to read four lessons: one each from the Old Testament, the Psalms, the New Testament epistles, and the gospels. But the prayer book allows for great flexibility in the number of lessons, as long as one of them is from the gospels. For weekday services often the celebrant will select one of the other readings, either from the Old or New Testaments, followed by the psalm, to accompany the gospel.

Since the reading from one of the gospels is the climax of this portion of the service, the church has long accompanied the proclamation of the gospel with special ceremonies. We stand to hear this reading, which is often proclaimed from the center of the church or nave. There is often a gospel procession, with acolytes holding torches and perhaps a thurifer swinging a thurible filled with burning incense as a reminder of our prayers rising to God as a fragrant offering. Often a psalm, known as the gradual psalm, or another hymn will be chanted before the proclamation of the gospel, as the acolytes and deacon or priest process to the place where the gospel will be read or sung. Since at least the third century, an alleluia verse has often preceded the gospel reading, usually combined with a passage from Scripture. Special responses are provided before and after the announcement of the reading. And by longstanding custom, only a deacon, priest, or bishop may read the passage from the gospel.

The sermon immediately follows the readings, thus emphasizing its intended purpose: to elaborate on and interpret the meaning of the Scripture passages just read. Sermons in the Episcopal Church are not generally an opportunity for the preacher to choose a topic of interest to him or her on which to elaborate. Rather, current events and pressing issues are normally discussed more fully in Sunday forums or other educational formats in the life of the congregation. This is not to say, however, that the sermon will be divorced from the daily lives of those who are listening. It is simply that the basis for the sermon is the interpretation of the Scriptures just heard, as the preacher seeks to articulate the meaning of those Scriptures in the light of our own experience of God.

The Creed, Prayers, and Confession

Although we have long been accustomed to reciting one of the creeds at this point in the service, during the first centuries of the church the eucharistic prayer itself was understood to be the creed, just as the prayers offered in the context of Jewish eucharistic meals recounted the story of God's acts of redemption in the history of the people of Israel. Separate creeds were developed in response to various heresies that arose during the first five or six centuries of the church's life, and these creeds were recited in the liturgies to remind continually new and old believers alike of what they believe.

The Nicene Creed was first compiled by the Council of Nicaea in 325, and is based on a baptismal profession of faith from the Eastern church. The creed was expanded later at the Council of Constantinople in 381 and finally adopted at the Council of Chalcedon in 451. At the time of the Reformation, some churches substituted the Apostles' Creed, since they believed it to be closer to Scripture, but Anglican prayer books retained the Nicene. (The Apostles' Creed is used at Morning and Evening Prayer.) In our 1979 prayer book, the creed is only required on Sundays and major feast days since the eucharistic prayers in this prayer book recount God's saving acts and "proclaim the faith in its fullness."[39]

People are often concerned that they cannot say all the words of the creed with complete conviction. Are they being hypocritical, they wonder, in repeating words they do not entirely understand or believe? This is a valid concern, of course. "Are we meant to shelve all our doubts and uncertainties as we recite the ancient words, then?" the liturgical theologian Marianne Micks asks. "By no means," she responds. "Worshiping God does not mean turning off our minds.

Quite the contrary. Within the context of faith all sorts of questions arise, and they should."[40] Micks goes on to describe the Nicene Creed as a kind of "punching bag"—"something to push against, at least, if not to fight" as a way of questioning and deepening our understanding of the faith.[41]

At their heart, however, the creeds recited in worship are not doctrines to be adhered to but proclamations of praise for what God has done. They summarize the Christian story, but also evoke our thanksgiving and worship. A wise friend once told me that when she cannot say parts of the creed with conviction she is content to let the church community gathered in worship affirm the whole of it for her, trusting that in time her understanding will change and deepen. She finds great strength in the fact that we usually begin the Nicene Creed with "*We* believe," not "*I* believe," for in the church community we carry each other along when we cannot affirm the creeds alone.

Since at least the second century, the prayers of the people have followed the hearing and proclamation of the Word of God, though the place of the intercessions has been shifted throughout the liturgy over the years. In the 1979 prayer book, the prayers of the people are restored to their earlier place in the eucharistic liturgy. Over the centuries these prayers of intercession have also taken a variety of forms. One of the earliest and most common is the litany, or bidding prayer, in which the leader mentions a specific intention and the people respond with a sentence or phrase, such as "Lord, have mercy" or "Lord, hear our prayer."

In the 1979 Book of Common Prayer we have six forms for the prayers of the people, as well as the prayer in Rite One intercessions familiarly known as the Prayer for the Whole State, since it is introduced with the words, "Let us pray for the whole state of Christ's Church and the world" (BCP 328). These forms are intended to be outlines and guides for further development and adaptation by those leading the prayers, not fixed and invariable texts.[42]

When making additions and changes to the intercessions, however, it is important to be aware of the basic format and purpose of the various prayer forms. Some are written in Elizabethan language, for example, for use with Rite One liturgies, and additions to the prayers should not be in sharp contrast. Likewise, confusion will result if litanies are interrupted in such a way that the people do not know when to respond. This most often occurs in Form III, when the leaders attempt to insert petitions in the midst of the sentences and responses rather than at the end, where such additions are usually invited.

No matter what form is used—one provided in the prayer book or one composed by a congregation—the prayers of intercession are to encompass six areas of concern: the church, the nation and "all in authority," the world, the local community, those who suffer or are in need, and the departed (BCP 383). As was the custom with the ancient litanies, the celebrant normally concludes the intercessions with a collect.

Following the prayers of intercession, we are given the opportunity to make a confession of sin (unless the service began with the Penitential Order, and thus the confession was done earlier). The confession is a rather late addition to the eucharistic liturgies, appearing during the Reformation as revisions of private prayers offered by priests during the Middle Ages. In the early church's liturgies, the general confession of sin was simply considered part of the recognition of and thanksgiving for God's redemptive actions in Christ. Or, as Marion Hatchett puts it, "Confession is the obverse of thanksgiving; to give thanks for redemption is to acknowledge one's sinfulness."[43] Thus in the 1979 prayer book the confession may be omitted on occasion, usually during particularly festive seasons of the church year.

The general confession should not be confused with private confession of individual sins, an important part of one's spiritual growth. (See chapter seven for a consideration of the Rite of Reconciliation in the Episcopal Church.) In this general confession we acknowledge our human condition of separation from God, our individual and corporate participation in the economic and social institutions through which we fail to love one another, and our common tendency toward self-centeredness and pride.

The first half of the eucharistic liturgy concludes with the exchange of the peace, a time of greeting one another in the name and peace of Christ. Though the exchange of "the kiss of peace" was an integral part of early baptismal liturgies and concluded the Liturgy of the Word, it was not included in most Reformation liturgies and has only recently been restored in most twentieth-century revisions of the Eucharist, including the 1979 prayer book. For many people, therefore, it was a new experience and not always a welcome one, since it seemed to intrude on the solemnity and privacy of their prayers. However, over time most Episcopalians have come to accept the peace and in many congregations it is a joyous, even boisterous time of fellowship and love.

There are many ways to exchange the peace, from a simple nod of the head to an enthusiastic embrace. The most common is a handshake or kiss on the cheek, accompanied by such words as "God's peace be with you." You normally exchange the peace with all of those sitting around you, though in smaller congregations or in a retreat setting you might well circulate the room to exchange the peace with everyone present.

THE HOLY COMMUNION

After exchanging the peace, we now come to the part of the service known as Holy Communion. The 1979 prayer book restores the most ancient name for this tradition of making Eucharist: the Great Thanksgiving. There are four primary actions within the Great Thanksgiving, and these are based on the actions of Jesus in the Last Supper as well as on the Jewish pattern of thanksgiving suppers: we offer bread and wine, we bless them, we break the bread, and we give the bread and wine to all who have gathered. In the church's vocabulary, these four actions of offering, blessing, breaking, and giving are called the offertory, consecration, fraction, and communion.

First, we offer. Bread and wine are brought up to the altar, usually by people from the congregation. The table is prepared by the deacon, whose actions symbolically convey the preparations we make before invited guests come to dinner. He or she lays out a clean white linen cloth, sets the table with cup and plate (called the chalice and paten), lays out enough bread or wafers for those gathered, and pours enough wine for all to share. The deacon will pour a bit of water into the wine, following an ancient custom that may have intended to recall the waters of baptism or simply to dilute the wine for drinking at a meal.

The Great Thanksgiving in our 1979 prayer book opens with a dialogue between the celebrant and the people, beginning with "The Lord be with you," to which we respond "And also with you." This opening dialogue is called the *Sursum corda* and is found in manuscripts as early as Hippolytus's *Apostolic Tradition*, though after the 1552 prayer book Anglicans lost sight of it until it was restored in 1979. This ancient dialogue echoes the Jewish forms of blessing of the time: "Lift up your hearts" was a command to stand; "Let us give thanks" was the celebrant's way of asking permission to offer thanksgivings on behalf of the people gathered.[44]

You may notice a paragraph soon after the opening dialogue that changes according to the season of the church year or the feast day on which that Eucharist is being celebrated. This paragraph is called the proper preface, and following ancient tradition this prayer book provides various prefaces for all the church seasons and a number of feast days. For example, the preface for the feast of All Saints in Rite One is:

Who, in the multitude of thy saints, hast compassed us about with so great a cloud of witnesses, that we, rejoicing in their fellowship, may run with patience the race that is set before us; and, together with them, may receive the crown of glory that fadeth not away. (BCP 347)

The priest then leads the people in a lengthy prayer of consecration known as the eucharistic prayer. Within both Rite One and Rite Two there are several alternative prayers of consecration: Eucharistic Prayer I and II in Rite One, both in Elizabethan language, and Eucharistic Prayer A, B, C, and D in Rite Two, all in contemporary language. The prayers in Rite One are fairly similar in tone and content, though Prayer II is simpler in language and richer in imagery, while those in Rite Two vary considerably. Prayer C, for example, was newly composed for this prayer book and calls for an extended dialogue between the celebrant and the people, using images that reflect a modern understanding of the world:

God of all power, Ruler of the Universe, you are worthy of glory and praise.
Glory to you for ever and ever.
At your command all things came to be: the vast expanse of interstellar space, galaxies, suns, the planets in their courses, and this fragile earth, our island home.
By your will they were created and have their being. (BCP 370)

Eucharistic Prayer D is adapted from the Liturgy of Saint Basil in the Eastern church, which is generally dated to the time of Basil the Great in the fourth century. This prayer focuses on the glorious majesty of the Lord:

It is truly right to glorify you, Father, and to give you thanks, for you alone are God, living and true, dwelling in light inaccessible from before time and for ever. . . . Countless throngs of angels stand before you to serve you night and day; and, beholding the glory of your presence, they offer you unceasing praise. (BCP 373)

This version of Basil's eucharistic prayer was developed by an ecumenical committee and is approved for use in several liturgical denominations, including the Roman Catholic, Lutheran, and Methodist churches.

Many congregations have developed patterns of using the various eucharistic prayers in the prayer book in order to introduce variety without creating confusion. For example, some will use the same prayer for a particular season of the church year—emphasizing Rite One's penitential flavor in Lent, perhaps, or the powerful images of the Incarnation in Rite Two's Prayer B during Advent. Other congregations prefer to use only one or two throughout the year, valuing the stability of repeating the same prayer each week and the freedom to pray that memorization can provide. Still others move freely among all the prayers week by week, and have developed a comfortable level of familiarity with them all.

You may encounter other alternative eucharistic prayers from the supplementary book *Enriching Our Worship 1*. These prayers offer more expansive images and language to speak to and about God and God's relationship with all creation. One of the eucharistic prayers included in that volume, for example, focuses on the wider universe as we know it today, as well as the motherly care of God for us:

We praise you and we bless you, holy and gracious God,
source of life abundant.
From before time you made ready the creation.
Your Spirit moved over the deep
and brought all things into being:
sun, moon, and stars;
earth, winds, and waters;
and every living thing.
You made us in your image,
and taught us to walk in your ways.
But we rebelled against you, and wandered far away;
and yet, as a mother cares for her children,
you would not forget us.
Time and again you called us
to live in the fullness of your love.[45]

At the end of the prayer of consecration, the priest will break the bread, an action known as the fraction. Practically speaking, the bread is broken so it can be distributed to the people. But the fraction also has a symbolic meaning: it is a solemn moment usually surrounded by silence, signifying the breaking of Christ's body on the cross for the redemption of the world. Then the bread and wine are immediately distributed to the people by the celebrant, deacon, and lay ministers who are appointed to serve that day.

In the Episcopal Church today we receive communion in a variety of ways. In some congregations you will go forward to the altar and kneel at an altar rail. In others, you may stand and receive in front of the altar or at various communion stations located throughout the church. At smaller weekday or retreat settings you may gather in a circle around the altar and pass the bread and cup to the person next to you after receiving.

Some people receive by eating the bread first and then drinking directly from the cup; others prefer to dip the wafer or morsel of bread into the wine and then consume the bread and wine together—a process known as "intinction." By ancient tradition we receive the bread in hands that are laid one on top of the other. The fourth-century bishop Cyril of Jerusalem instructed those preparing for baptism, "Do not come with your hands stretched or your fingers separated, but make your left hand a throne for the right which is to receive a king."[46] The custom of intinction was introduced in the Middle Ages as an attempt to discourage people from secretly taking away the wafer given to them for superstitious practices, though today the practice is usually done more for hygienic concerns about drinking from a common cup.

During communion, and while the servers clear the table, hymns or anthems are usually sung by the congregation or choir. A number of beautiful hymns about the theology and experience of receiving the Eucharist have been written over the centuries, and as always the music and poetry of hymns has a tremendous power to express what cannot easily be put into words. One of the most ancient hymns about the Eucharist, adapted from a second-century Greek text, is included in our hymnal:

Father, we thank thee who hast planted
thy holy Name within our hearts.
Knowledge and faith and life immortal
Jesus thy Son to us imparts.

As grain, once scattered on the hillsides,
was in this broken bread made one,
so from all lands thy Church be gathered
into thy kingdom by thy Son.[47]

We then conclude with one of the postcommunion prayers, a custom that seems to have been well established by the fourth century and has been continued ever since. The postcommunion prayers in the 1979 prayer book not only offer thanks for the gifts we have just received, but also focus on the multilayered meaning of what we have just done in offering thanks as "members incorporate in the mystical body of thy Son, the blessed company of all faithful people" (BCP 339). They also ask God to "send us now into the world in peace, and grant us strength and courage to love and serve you with gladness and singleness of heart" (BCP 365) as we offer our ministries as Christians within the church and to the world.

The priest or bishop may then bless the people, using one of the many options gathered throughout the centuries from Scripture and from Jewish and Christian tradition. The blessing often concludes with the priest or bishop making the sign of the cross over the people while saying a sentence taken from the 1549 Book of Common Prayer: "And the blessing of God Almighty, the Father, the Son, and the Holy Ghost, be amongst you and remain with you always." A number of new blessings have also been written or translated that use a broad variety of images and can be found in *The Book of Occasional Services* or *Enriching Our Worship 1*, such as this blessing from the Celtic tradition:

God's Blessing be with you,
Christ's peace be with you,
the Spirit's outpouring be with you,
now and always. *Amen.*[48]

Finally, the service concludes with the dismissal. The earliest dismissal we know of, from the fourth-century *Apostolic Constitutions*, is "Depart in peace," spoken by the deacon, to which the people would respond, "In the name of Christ." The earlier English prayer books dropped the dismissal, and the 1979 book is the first to restore it, providing several forms of the dismissal from early and medieval liturgical traditions.

Volumes have been written over the centuries concerning the meaning of the Eucharist, and the experience of giving thanks and sharing a meal of bread and wine in memory of Christ has been shaped by developments in theology in each generation. The church has focused on the dimension of thanksgiving for all God has done for us in Christ; on the mystery of God's grace and presence in this sacrament of bread and wine; on the ways it nurtures and sustains our common life in the community of believers; and on its anticipa-tion of the heavenly banquet, the second coming of Christ, and the fulfillment of the kingdom of God on earth as it is in heaven. At its heart, however, the Eucharist is a simple act of love given and received. In the eating of bread and the drinking of wine mingled with water, we share in the humble, human means through which we daily receive the grace through which we were made new crea-tures and "marked as Christ's own for ever" in our baptism. The liturgical scholar Dom Gregory Dix describes it well:

> At the heart of it all is the eucharistic action, a thing of an absolute simplicity—the taking, blessing, breaking and giving of bread and the taking, blessing and giving of a cup of wine and water, as these were first done with their new meaning by a young Jew before and after supper with His friends on the night before He died. Soon it was simplified further, by leaving out the sup-per and combining the double grouping before and after it into a single rite. So the four-action Shape of the Liturgy was found at the end of the first century. He had told His friends to do this henceforward with the new meaning of "for the *anamnesis*" of Him, and they have done it always since.[49]

QUESTIONS FOR REFLECTION AND DISCUSSION

1. Do you remember the first time you received Holy Communion? What was it like? What meanings has the Eucharist held for you since then?

2. In what ways are the meals you have shared among family and friends similar to a Christian Eucharist? Are there family gatherings that particularly stand out for you as occasions of thanksgiving and remembrance?

3. Turn to the various eucharistic prayers in the prayer book (BCP 333–36, 340–43, 361–63, 367–75). What common words or images do you see in all of the prayers? How do the prayers differ?

Praying throughout the Day
The Daily Office

Blessed are you, O Lord, the God of our fathers, creator of the changes of day and night, giving rest to the weary, renewing the strength of those who are spent, bestowing upon us occasions of song in the evening. As you have protected us in the day that is past, so be with us in the coming night; keep us from every sin, every evil, and every fear; for you are our light and salvation, and the strength of our life. To you be glory for endless ages. Amen.

(BCP 113)

The sunlight is just beginning to filter through the curtain in the young man's bedroom as he stirs at the sound of the alarm clock. It is morning, the dawn of a new day. Rubbing his eyes, he finds his slippers and heads downstairs to brew some coffee. In a few moments the sizzling, rich aroma fills the air. Breathing deeply, he gathers his steaming mug, his prayer book, and his Bible, and heads for his favorite armchair. He opens the well-worn Book of Common Prayer and selects one of the opening sentences, saying aloud: "Send out your light and your truth, that they may lead me, and bring me to your holy hill and to your dwelling." It is time to begin the day. It is time for Morning Prayer.

Later in the day, he drives to the church parking lot before returning home. He is weary and preoccupied with the stresses of a difficult day at work, but as he enters the church, half lit in the fading afternoon sunlight, and stands for a moment in the cool, quiet space, he feels his tensed muscles begin to relax. The side chapel lights are on, and several people are gathered there, sitting quietly with their eyes closed or gazing reflectively at the cross above the altar. He finds a seat just as the priest enters, and everyone stands. "Let my prayer be set forth in your sight as incense, the lifting up of my hands as the evening sacrifice," the priest begins. As the service continues, his perspective begins to shift; the events of the day that has passed come into focus, now set in the context of prayer and worship. "The day thou gavest, Lord, is ended, the darkness falls at thy behest," he sings, hearing their voices grow stronger and less tentative as the stone walls carry their song to heaven and fill the small chapel with music. He is glad he has come. He is glad to be part of this community of prayer.

THE ORIGINS OF THE DAILY OFFICE

Although Christians very early began to meet regularly for Eucharist on Sundays, they also were steeped in a religious tradition that called them to prayer and the repetition of the songs of Judaism several times throughout the day. The Daily Office as we have it now in the Episcopal prayer book evolved from the ancient Jewish and thus early Christian practice of setting aside certain times of the day for prayer and song, especially the reading and chanting of psalms.

Some of these hours of prayer were kept as public or family services in the synagogue or in homes; others were times of individual devotions. For Christians, the third, sixth, and ninth hours (9 A.M., 12 noon, and 3 P.M.) were associated with events that occurred during Jesus' passion. The church added to these two other hours of prayer: midnight, a time of praise for the God of all creation, and cockcrow or sunrise, a time to remember the disciples' denial of Christ and the hope of resurrection.

During the rapid growth of Christianity in the fourth century under Constantine, weekday services became more frequent and formal. The principal morning and evening services, called Lauds and Vespers, were held in a number of congregations and included various readings and the singing of psalms, as well as intercessions and prayers. Particularly in the cathedrals, these liturgies grew to be rather elaborate. These "very churchy, somewhat vulgar, clergy-dominated" services with their incense, vestments, and rituals have been memorably described as "reasonably brief, colorful, ceremonious, odiferous, and full of movement."[50]

At the same time, the monasteries were also developing a pattern of liturgies for use throughout the day, based on the reading of Scripture and the singing of the entire Psalter. These liturgies for the hours of prayer were called "offices," from the Latin word *opus*, or "work." The daily offices were thus considered the "work of God" by those who prayed them day after day.

The monastic offices tended to be more austere ceremonies, meditative and even ascetic in their tone and simplicity. They were often led by monks who were lay members of the church rather than clergy. The monastic practice of reading the books of the Bible "in course" (straight through from beginning to end) and of regularly chanting the Psalms in their entirety—in some places as often as every day, in others every week or fortnight—became associated with the Daily Office at this time, and has remained an important foundation for the daily hours of prayer to this day.

The monasteries of the early Middle Ages developed seven daily offices said as a community in the chapel: Matins (at midnight or cockcrow), Lauds (the public morning service), Prime (6 A.M.), Terce (9 A.M.), Sext (12 noon), None (3 P.M.), and Vespers (the public evening service). Compline was said in the monks' private rooms just before retiring to bed.

During the later Middle Ages the Daily Office became increasingly the obligation and practice of monks and clergy, although private devotional books called the *Book of Hours* or *Primer* were developed for those laypeople in the congregations who could read. Over time the monastic offices began to be grouped together: Matins, Lauds, and Prime became Matins; Vespers and Compline were combined into a sung service called Evensong.

These combined daily offices from the monasteries and cathedrals of the Middle Ages were revised and incorporated in the prayer books of many of the Reformation churches, usually as a morning and an evening service. Cranmer's first Book of Common Prayer certainly reflects elements from both the cathedral and monastic services, although he leaned more heavily on the monastic offices. Cranmer believed them to be "the first original ground" of the church's common prayers, especially in their simplicity and emphasis on the reading of the entire Bible in the language of the people so that they "have profit by hearing the same," without leaving out certain portions or "breaking one piece thereof from another."[51] The Daily Office as we now have it still tends more toward monastic simplicity, though new to this prayer book is a cathedral-style office for evening, An Order of Worship for the Evening, which incorporates incense and candlelighting in its ceremonial.

THE DAILY OFFICE IN THE EPISCOPAL CHURCH TODAY

In the 1979 Book of Common Prayer we have both Rite One and Rite Two versions of Morning and Evening Prayer. New to this prayer book are the offices for prayers for noonday (a combination of the monastic offices of Terce, Sext, and None) and Compline (based on the fourth-century monastic order of prayers before going to bed at night). Thus the 1979 prayer book provides a fourfold Daily Office for individuals, families, and congregations to use as the basis for their daily devotions, their reading of Scripture, and their prayers to God. All of them may be led entirely by laypersons as well as by clergy.

From its beginnings, the Daily Office has centered on the reading of the Bible, the Word of God. To this end, a Daily Office Lectionary is included in our prayer book, with sequential readings for daily Morning and Evening Prayer, including Sundays, given in a two-year cycle. In this lectionary the New Testament will be read through twice during the two years, and the Old Testament once. The Daily Office Lectionary provides three readings for each day, one each from the Old and New Testaments, and a third from one of the gospels. When and in what combination these lessons are read depends on how many offices are being kept that day, though the Old Testament lesson is normally read in the morning. If only one of the offices is being kept that day, then all three lessons are read at that time.

The lectionary also provides for the reading of the Psalter over a seven-week period, with selections of psalms appropriate for morning and evening. However, for those who prefer to read the Psalms more frequently and in their entirety, the 1979 prayer book has retained the 1549 prayer book's division of the Psalter into portions that allow the entire Psalter to be read once a month. If you turn to the Psalter in the 1979 Book of Common Prayer, above each psalm number you will find in italic printing the divisions for thirty days, morning and evening. The psalms to be read at Morning Prayer on the ninth day of every month, for example, are Psalms 44, 45, and 46; those for Evening Prayer on that day are Psalms 47, 48, and 49 (see BCP 645–50).

The Psalter in the 1979 prayer book is a careful updating of Coverdale's revision of the Psalter in the Great Bible of 1539, which was used in the first prayer book of 1549. Our Psalter has been revised in light of modern Hebrew scholarship but has tried to preserve the beautiful rhythms and syntax of Coverdale's version. It is still printed in lines of poetry in order to retain the original Hebrew forms and to help with the chanting of the psalms in our services.[52]

You will still find a number of Episcopal churches today celebrating Morning Prayer on Sunday mornings, though it is usually not the principal service of the morning. Some follow the tradition of English cathedrals in offering Evensong on Sunday afternoons. Many congregations also offer services of Morning and Evening Prayer on a regular basis throughout the week. Some likewise include other offices during the church year, such as praying Compline together after a Lenten evening program or noonday prayer in the midst of an annual vestry retreat or Advent quiet day.

It is difficult to know, of course, to what extent the Daily Office is kept at home by individual Episcopalians today. Many find the formal structure it provides for daily prayer and the reading of Scripture to be an invaluable foundation for spiritual growth, and the keeping of at least one of the offices each day is the basis for the regular nurture of their spiritual life. Others choose to pray the offices more occasionally, and find their life reordered and grounded by the traditional words that have been spoken, prayed, and heard for centuries by countless numbers of the saints. Still others use the prayer book's offices as an outline for their daily devotions, and use their creativity to incorporate prayers, readings, and practices from

Christian and other religious traditions, such as Celtic prayers and Eastern meditation or body prayer.

No matter what pattern of daily prayer one chooses to practice, the regular practice of offering prayer throughout the day is of great importance for Christians. In one of Phyllis Tickle's introductions to her several-volume adaptation of the Daily Office for modern Christians, she eloquently summarizes the intended purpose of praying the office:

> While the words and ordering of the prayers of the Divine Hours have changed and changed again over the centuries, that purpose and characterization have remained constant. Other prayers may be petitionary or intercessory or valedictory or any number of other things, but the Liturgy of the Hours remains an act of offering . . . offering by the creature to the Creator. The fact that the creature grows strong and his or her faith more sinewy and efficacious as a result of keeping the hours is a by-product (albeit a desirable one) of that practice and not its purpose.[53]

No doubt everyone who prays the Daily Office regularly has found times when the repetition of these prayers has seemed empty or meaningless, and Tickle's assertion that the office is an offering to God rather than a means for feeling especially "spiritual" can be a steadying reminder through those dry seasons. Praying the Daily Office can thus be an antidote to our tendency to pray only when we feel like it. It is thus similar to the work of marriage or professions or other significant commitments in our lives: our faith is shaped by maturity, stability, and the many dimensions of deep and abiding love through our offering of the daily *opus Dei*, the work of God.

MORNING PRAYER

The primary purpose of Morning Prayer is the praise and adoration of God at break of day. The name itself once conveyed this meaning: Lauds, the Latin name of the monastic office that forms the basis for our office of Morning Prayer, comes from the *Laudate* psalms of praise (such as Psalms 148–150) that were recited frequently in the medieval office. "Lord, open our lips," the office begins after the long silence of the night, "And our mouth shall proclaim your praise" (BCP 80).

The psalm that follows—called the Invitatory Psalm because it invites the people to prayer and praise of God—is either Psalm 95 or Psalm 100, called by their Latin names *Venite* and *Jubilate* for the first words in each psalm. The *Jubilate* begins:

Be joyful in the Lord, all you lands;
serve the Lord with gladness
and come before his presence with a song. (BCP 82)

During the Great Fifty Days of Easter, and particularly during Easter Week, a canticle called the *Pascha nostrum* (Christ our Passover) may be sung or said instead. It is a combination of several passages from the letters of Saint Paul concerning the death and resurrection of Christ, and was compiled by Archbishop Cranmer in the 1549 Book of Common Prayer for use during a procession prior to Morning Prayer.

The reading or preferably singing of the psalms—they were the first Jewish hymnal—follows the Invitatory. As noted earlier, it is possible either to recite the selection of psalms assigned in the Daily Office Lectionary or to follow the outline of divisions for each month provided in the 1979 prayer book's Psalter. There are a number of traditional ways of reciting the psalms. Sometimes you will hear them read responsively by half-verse, meaning that half the congregation will read the first line up to the asterisk, and the other half will respond with the second line after the asterisk. Sometimes a cantor or reader will say or sing the first half, and the congregation will respond with the second. In monastic or retreat settings there will often be a breathing space of silence at the asterisk as well. And of course, the psalms may simply be read in unison.

A large body of plainsong (the traditional modal music of the Roman rite sung in the early medieval church), metrical, and Anglican chant forms has been developed over the centuries for the singing of the psalms, enhancing the meditative dimension of these timeless prayers to God. Some are quite elaborate and intended to be sung by trained musicians, but many are simple enough for even the nonmusical and tone-deaf to enjoy singing. Chants that include antiphons are sometimes used when a choir is present: the congregation joins in the singing of the antiphon at the beginning and end of the psalm, or as a refrain after each verse or a group of verses.

After the psalms at least one and perhaps two or three passages from the Bible will be read. The lectionary provides for three readings each day, and it is up to the individual's or leader's discretion as to how many to use for a particular service, though the instructions concerning the Daily Office Lectionary direct that "when more than one Reading is used at an Office the first is always from the Old Testament (or the Apocrypha)" (BCP 934). The instructions also note that "any Reading may be lengthened at discretion," thus encouraging people to use these times of daily prayer as an opportunity to expand their knowledge of the Scriptures by setting a particular passage into its larger context.

After each reading, one of the canticles is sung or said. Like the psalms, a canticle is a portion of Scripture that is set in verses designed to be sung. The 1549 Book of Common Prayer provided only three canticles for Matins, but our current revision expands the offerings to twenty-one. Some may be used at any time of the year; others are especially appropriate at certain seasons of the church year, such as A Song of Penitence during Lent or The Song of Moses for the Easter season. A table offering suggestions for which day of the week to use each canticle is also provided (BCP 144).

Canticles one through seven are given in the traditional Elizabethan language of Rite One and eight through twenty-one are in contemporary English. But they all may be adapted to contemporary or traditional language, depending on whether the office is being said in Rite One or Rite Two. All but two of the canticles are taken from both the Old and New Testaments, as well as the books of the Apocrypha, including Exodus, Isaiah, the Song of the Three Young Men, Luke, and the Revelation to John. Canticles twenty and twenty-one, the *Gloria in excelsis* and the *Te Deum laudamus*, are not passages from Scripture but are included as ancient hymns of praise from the church's tradition, dating to at least the fourth century.

After the lessons and canticles we proclaim our faith by reciting the creed, using the Apostles' Creed rather than the Nicene Creed used at the Eucharist. This ancient baptismal affirmation of faith contains the responses the candidates would make to three questions concerning their belief in God the Father, God the Son, and God the Holy Spirit. This baptismal creed has been associated with the Daily Office since at least the eighth century, and its use "reminds us of our common baptism as the ground of our common prayer."[54]

A section called The Prayers follows the creed in Morning Prayer, and includes the Lord's Prayer and one of two sets of suffrages— petitions in the form of versicles said by the officiant (identified as "V" in the prayer book) and responses said by the people in the congregation (identified as "R"). At least one and usually two or three collects follow, as well as a prayer for mission. The people are then given the opportunity freely to make their own intercessions, petitions, and thanksgivings, either silently or aloud. A hymn often precedes or follows these free-form prayers.

The concluding prayer is one of two prayers of thanksgiving. The General Thanksgiving is a prayer composed in the seventeenth century giving thanks for "our creation, preservation, and all the blessings of this life" (BCP 101). The Prayer of Saint Chrysostom was not actually written by the fourth-century bishop John Chrysostom, but was adapted by Archbishop Cranmer from a Latin translation of an ancient Eastern liturgy. It is well loved by many Anglicans throughout the world since it expresses our conviction that common prayer is at the heart of our life together:

> Almighty God, you have given us grace at this time with one accord to make our common supplication to you; and you have promised through your well-beloved Son that when two or three are gathered together in his Name you will be in the midst of them: Fulfill now, O Lord, our desires and petitions as may be best for us; granting us in this world knowledge of your truth, and in the age to come life everlasting. *Amen.* (BCP 102)

The office concludes with a simple traditional dismissal, to which alleluias may be added during the Easter season, and a sentence from one of the letters in the New Testament affirming our trust in God's abiding presence and grace as we begin another day.

Although the value and importance of the 1979 prayer book's restoration of the celebration of the Eucharist to its place on Sunday mornings can hardly be questioned, one of the consequences of this shift has been the loss of Morning Prayer in the life of many congregations. Not too many decades ago Episcopalians would have been more familiar with the service of Morning Prayer than with Holy Communion; the reverse is certainly true today, to the extent that many long-time church members, including liturgical scholars such as Leonel Mitchell, have lamented that "it is not at all clear that the contemporary Church either sees a need for the Daily Office or is willing to make a place for it in its liturgical life."[55]

One solution for congregations is to use Morning Prayer as the Liturgy of the Word prior to Holy Communion. This custom dates back at least to the sixteenth century, when Archbishop Grindal directed Anglican congregations to celebrate Sunday services that included Morning Prayer, the Litany, and everything prior to the intercessions. On those Sundays in which the Lord's Supper was celebrated—once a week in a few places, once a month in others, and once every quarter in most—the eucharistic prayer and communion would then follow. Many congregations today find this practice of using Morning Prayer in the context of the Eucharist is one way of offering Episcopalians the best of both worlds: the beauty and substance of the canticles, lessons, psalms, and prayers of Morning Prayer as well as the solid and ancient tradition of celebrating the Eucharist every Sunday.

NOONDAY PRAYER

An Order of Service for Noonday is new to the Book of Common Prayer in the 1979 edition. Based on the midday monastic "little offices" of Terce, Sext, and None, as well as the Jewish and early Christian practice of pausing throughout the day for private or family prayers, this simple, brief office is intended for public as well as private use. Episcopalians today most often pray this office just prior to the lunch break when we have gathered for meetings, conferences, quiet days, or retreats, but the office is also appropriately offered in the late morning and early afternoon.

The office begins with an opening versicle that was used at these times of prayer since at least the sixth century: "O God, make speed to save us," the officiant begins; "O Lord, make haste to help us," the people respond. The psalms that are printed within the office are the ones traditionally associated with these midday offices, though the rubrics also list others that are suitable for prayer at this time of day. In the same way, several brief verses from the Old and New Testaments are printed within the office or "some other suitable passage of Scripture" may be read. All of the readings focus on the activity of God in the world and in human lives, and our response in thanksgiving and praise: "The LORD has done great things for us, and we are glad indeed," Psalm 126 proclaims (BCP 105).

A brief homily or meditation may be given after the lessons. The prayers then follow, beginning with the *Kyrie* and the Lord's Prayer. The collects focus on the events of Jesus' passion that took place at noonday, as well as the mission of the church in proclaiming the gospel "that all nations may come and worship" this Savior (BCP 107). Free intercessions may then be offered, either silently or aloud, and the office concludes with the simple and ancient dismissal, "Let us bless the Lord"; "Thanks be to God" (BCP 107).

EVENING PRAYER

Along with the Eucharist and Morning Prayer, Evening Prayer is one of "the regular services appointed for public worship in this Church" (BCP 13). Since the Middle Ages the monastic office of Vespers, on which our Evening Prayer is based, has popularly been called Evensong, and you will still hear that name commonly used today when the psalms, canticles, and prayers of Evening Prayer are sung rather than said.

The order for Evening Prayer is structured very much like that for Morning Prayer, with the opening sentences and optional confession followed by the reading or singing of psalms and the reading of at least one lesson from Scripture. The Invitatory for Evening Prayer is the *Phos hilaron*, "O Gracious Light," an ancient hymn that accompanied the lighting of candles. Already by the fourth century Basil the Great could refer to this beautiful hymn extolling Jesus as the "gracious Light" who is the "pure brightness of the everliving Father in heaven" as a cherished tradition of the church.[56] The words of the *Phos hilaron* also express well the purpose of Evening Prayer:

Now as we come to the setting of the sun,
and our eyes behold the vesper light,
we sing your praises, O God: Father, Son, and Holy Spirit.

You are worthy at all times to be praised by happy voices,
O Son of God, O Giver of life,
and to be glorified through all the worlds. (BCP 118)

At this office we gather in the evening to offer praise to God for the day that is past, as well as to recognize that although we often fail to offer that praise with "happy voices," God remains worthy of our adoration and worship.

The traditional canticles for Evening Prayer are the *Magnificat* (The Song of Mary) and the *Nunc dimittis* (The Song of Simeon), but any of the canticles printed in the order for Morning Prayer may also be used. Musical settings in great abundance have been composed in the Anglican Church for these two canticles, and have been regularly sung in cathedrals and parish churches in England and elsewhere for centuries.

The first set of suffrages in Evening Prayer is the same as those for Morning Prayer; the second set is new to the 1979 prayer book and is based on a litany from the evening office in the Eastern churches. The collects speak of our desire for pardon, peace, and protection, and our confidence in God's light remaining as the darkness of evening gathers, as in this collect based on the gospel story of the risen Jesus' appearance to the disciples on the road to Emmaus:

Lord Jesus, stay with us, for evening is at hand and the day is past; be our companion in the way, kindle our hearts, and awaken hope, that we may know you as you are revealed in Scripture and the breaking of bread. (BCP 124)

The prayers for mission and intercession likewise ask for God's abiding presence among all people throughout the night, as in this prayer of Augustine of Hippo:

> Keep watch, dear Lord, with those who work, or watch, or weep this night, and give your angels charge over those who sleep. Tend the sick, Lord Christ; give rest to the weary, bless the dying, soothe the suffering, pity the afflicted, shield the joyous; and all for your love's sake. (BCP 124)

Evening Prayer concludes with the same prayers of thanksgiving for God's mercy and grace found in Morning Prayer.

AN ORDER OF WORSHIP FOR THE EVENING

This evening service focusing on the blessing of lamps or candles as they are lit in the darkness (known as the *lucernarium*) is new to the 1979 prayer book, but it is one of the most ancient liturgies of the church. Christians in the early church followed the Jewish custom of blessing the light at the evening meal, and by the second century they kept a simple evening service of *lucernarium* that also included prayers, the singing of psalms, and sometimes an *agape* meal. In the Roman church of the early Middle Ages the service was transferred to the cathedrals and church buildings, but eventually was replaced by the monastic offices for the evening. Christians continued to offer a blessing of light in their homes in some places, however. Two books published during the reign of Queen Elizabeth, *A Book of Christian Prayers* and a collection of private prayers by the Anglican bishop Lancelot Andrewes, both contained thanksgivings for light to be prayed in the evening.

Although this evening office is offered less frequently than Evening Prayer, the beauty and timeless grace of the prayers and rituals of this service have greatly enriched Episcopalians' experience of evening worship. The service as we have it in our prayer book is more of an outline with prayers and suggested readings provided that can be used in any number of ways and places: as a "complete rite in place of Evening Prayer," as an introduction to an evening service, or as "the prelude to an evening meal or other activity" (BCP 108). In a simplified form it is easily kept at home as well, and can become a significant part of a family's life of prayer.

The service opens in the dark with the words, "Light and peace, in Jesus Christ our Lord" (BCP 109). A very brief passage from Scripture follows, and then the officiant offers one of the Prayers for Light. The four prayers provided here are all from various liturgical traditions within the church. The first prayer is from the eleventh-century Ambrosian prayer book, for example:

> Almighty God, we give you thanks for surrounding us, as day-light fades, with the brightness of the vesper light; and we implore you of your great mercy that, as you enfold us with the radiance of this light, so you would shine into our hearts the brightness of your Holy Spirit; through Jesus Christ our Lord. *Amen.* (BCP 110)

The second Prayer for Light is from a Celtic prayer of Saint Columbanus, while the third is a prayer from the Mozarabic breviary and the fourth has long appeared in most books of prayers in the Roman and English churches in the West. Even when time or occasion does not allow for the entire order for the service to be used, one of these calming prayers for light can accompany the lighting of a candle for prayer, for a meal, or simply for the marking of the time of transition to the evening.

At this point in the service the candles are lit. Any number and type of candles can be used, depending on the space and occasion, from clusters of candles on and around the altar and church building to a single taper on the dinner table. The traditional candle-lighting hymn also included in Evening Prayer, the *Phos hilaron*, then follows.

A number of options are given for how the service proceeds, depending on the occasion. Two prayers that are especially suitable for the evening are provided for use before the final blessing. The first of the prayers (which is quoted at the beginning of this chapter) is an adaptation of one of the private prayers of Bishop Lancelot Andrewes, while the second is from the Taizé monastic community in France. The second is especially appropriate when incense has been part of the ceremonial surrounding the lighting of the lamps or candles:

Almighty, everlasting God, let our prayer in your sight be as incense, the lifting up of our hands as the evening sacrifice. Give us grace to behold you, present in your Word and Sacraments, and to recognize you in the lives of those around us. Stir up in us the flame of that love which burned in the heart of your Son as he bore his passion, and let it burn in us to eternal life and to the ages of ages. *Amen.* (BCP 113)

COMPLINE

Like the Order of Worship for the Evening, the ancient night office of Compline is also new to this prayer book. It has quickly become a favorite office for both individuals and gatherings of Christians at retreats and conferences, and following times of parish study or evening meetings. Compline originated in the psalms and prayers said by the monks in their beds before retiring for the night, and over time it developed into a more formal night office said by small groups of Christians in the late evening.

The office begins with a simple confession of sin to acknowledge our failings of the day that has passed and to receive God's forgiveness before retiring to bed. One of the three night psalms that Benedict of Nursia directed his monks to recite "straightforwardly without antiphons"[57] is then said, and a brief passage from Scripture follows. A hymn may then be sung, and a number of evening hymns in *The Hymnal 1982* are appropriate here. One ancient hymn traditionally associated with Compline is "To you before the close of day":

To you before the close of day,
Creator of all things, we pray
that in your constant clemency
our guard and keeper you would be.

Save us from troubled, restless sleep,
from all ill dreams your children keep;

so calm our minds that fears may cease
and rested bodies wake in peace.[58]

The prayers and collects in Compline are brief and focus on
God's protection through the coming night, and on Christ as our
light in the darkness. They all reflect the timeless grace and simple
cadence of Western prayers from the early Roman tradition:

Be present, O merciful God, and protect us through the hours of
this night, so that we who are wearied by the changes and chances
of this life may rest in your eternal changelessness; through Jesus
Christ our Lord. *Amen.* (BCP 133)

Compline concludes with the canticle the Song of Simeon, this
time accompanied by an antiphon traditionally used in this office:
"Guide us waking, O Lord, and guard us sleeping; that awake we
may watch with Christ, and asleep we may rest in peace." This comforting antiphon is well worth committing to memory for use
throughout the night; in our family we often say it as part of our
nightly tuck-in ritual with our oldest son.

DAILY DEVOTIONS
Although all of the liturgies of the Daily Office can be used privately as well as publicly, at least since the time of Queen Elizabeth
the prayer book has often been accompanied by collections of devotions to be used by individuals or families. The 1979 Book of
Common Prayer likewise includes a section of Daily Devotions for
use in our homes. These forms are a revision of prayers published in
1705 by Edmund Gibson, later bishop of London, for use in his
parish in Lambeth.

Devotions are provided for the morning, noon, early evening,
and "at the close of day." They can thus be used when you do not
have sufficient time for one of the longer daily offices, or when a
shorter, flexible service is helpful (as when praying them with children). The basic structure for these devotions follows that of the
Daily Office, with psalms, readings, and prayers. They can be as
elaborate or as simple as needed, and great flexibility is allowed in the

selection of lessons and prayers. All the selections are also included in the orders for Morning and Evening Prayer, noonday prayer, and Compline.

The portion of Psalm 113 provided for prayer at noon perhaps summarizes best the primary purpose for all forms of prayer throughout the day, whether elaborate cathedral services with magnificent anthems sung by a choir or the whispered prayers of a child before bed: "From the rising of the sun to its going down let the Name of the LORD be praised" (BCP 138).

QUESTIONS FOR REFLECTION AND DISCUSSION

1. In what formal and informal ways do you pray daily? When do you pray regularly during the day? Do you usually pray alone or with others?

2. Have you tried praying the Daily Office or keeping a fixed time of daily prayer? If so, how did it fit into your normal schedule? What changes did you need to make to maintain the practice? How long did you stay with it? If you no longer are praying daily, what prompted you to stop?

3. If you are not currently praying the Daily Office regularly, would you like to give it a try? How can you envision incorporating one or more of the offices into your daily life? Try praying one of the offices daily for a week, and then reflect on how this commitment affected your understanding of prayer.

Marking the Seasons
The Church Year

Assist us mercifully with your help, O Lord God of our salvation,
that we may enter with joy upon the contemplation of those mighty
acts, whereby you have given us life and immortality; through Jesus
Christ our Lord. Amen.

(Liturgy of the Palms, BCP 270)

She had waited for this day for so long and now it was finally here. Christmas is my favorite time of the year, she thought; I love singing Christmas carols and opening all the presents and decorating the Christmas tree and having special treats to eat and seeing people being nice to each other. She looked around at all the other children crowded around the door to the church, waiting to walk in line down the aisle for the pageant. Jason, her younger brother, had to be a sheep again this year, and he was pouting but still interested in seeing what was going to happen. He was too young to remember it all from last year. Her best friend Isabelle was one of the angels, and like most of the other angels, Isabelle loved dressing in a fluffy white dress with wings and wearing a halo on her head.

She peered over the heads of the younger children to look into the church toward the wooden stable that had been set up in front of the altar. This was the first year she had ever played Mary in the pageant, and she was a bit nervous and awed by the responsibility.

Maybe the real Mary felt that way, too, she thought. Playing the part of Mary made her feel older, somehow, and maybe even a little closer to God. Her life seemed a little more meaningful, like what she did was part of a bigger plan God had for her and for everyone. She remembered all the different roles she had played over the years: shepherd, sheep, angel, even the first half of a donkey. Each one of us is different, she realized suddenly as she looked around her, but each of us has an important part in God's play. Maybe that's what Christmas is all about.

THE CHURCH YEAR

All of the liturgical services of the church such as baptism, Eucharist, and the Daily Office take place in the context of a larger structure called the church year. The church year is divided into seasons: Advent, Christmas, Epiphany, Lent, Holy Week, Easter, and Pentecost, with the rest of the weeks numbered sequentially in the Season after Pentecost. Within each season there are a number of feasts and fasts intended to mark a particular event, person, or aspect of the Christian faith, teaching us the content of our faith and giving us a way to celebrate what we believe year after year.[59]

You will find two sections in the 1979 Book of Common Prayer that provide information about the church year. An outline of all the seasons and feasts of the church year is given in the section at the beginning of the prayer book called The Calendar of the Church Year (BCP 15–33). The actual liturgies for several of the main services of Lent and Holy Week, including Ash Wednesday, Palm Sunday, Maundy Thursday, Good Friday, Holy Saturday, and the Easter Vigil, are found in a section called Proper Liturgies for Special Days (BCP 263–95). *The Book of Occasional Services* also contains supplemental materials for keeping the church year, including seasonal blessings, Advent and Christmas festivals of lessons and carols, an order for the Lenten office of Tenebrae, and blessings for use in our homes at Epiphany and Easter.

There are many approaches to living out the church year, of course, but the simplest is to see the church year in historical terms, as we follow the events in Jesus' life, especially his death and resurrection, and some of the events that took place in the early church.

Thus we begin the church year with Advent preparations for Jesus' birth at Christmas and the coming of the magi at Epiphany, and move on to the days before Jesus' death on Good Friday, his resurrection on Easter Sunday, and his ascension forty days later. We then finally turn to the coming of the Spirit and the birth of the church at Pentecost.

Even in the midst of these historical commemorations, however, it is important to note that we also keep these seasons as a way of understanding and participating in the eternal and mysterious meaning of the holy days of the calendar, beyond all time and human history. Just as in the Eucharist we remember Jesus' Last Supper with his disciples as well as celebrate his real and living presence with us in the breaking of the bread on this day, so in the seasons of the church year we both remember the events of Jesus' life and know that the significance of those events—that God chose to become human so we might no longer be separated from the divine love by our sins—is true in our own lives today. In the words of the liturgical scholar and priest Massey Shepherd, "The Christian year is a mystery through which every moment and all times and seasons of this life are transcended and fulfilled in that reality which is beyond time."[60]

Over the centuries an abundance of traditions have developed around the celebrations of the seasons, feasts, and fasts of the Christian calendar. One tradition widely practiced in the Episcopal Church today to mark the change of seasons is the use of color. You will probably notice that as you move through the church year the color of the vestments worn by the clergy and the fabrics used to adorn the altar area will change according to the season. The palette of colors we use today includes green, red, purple, white, and blue, but the association of certain colors with certain seasons is a fairly recent practice, dating from the late nineteenth and early twentieth centuries.

When you attend a service in an Episcopal Church, you can usually determine which season or feast day is being celebrated that day by checking the service leaflet or bulletin. It will indicate which Sunday within the season that particular day is (such as "The Second Sunday of Advent") or the name of the feast being celebrated (such as "The Presentation of Our Lord Jesus Christ in the Temple"). You can also gather clues by the color of the vestments and altar hangings (blue or purple for Advent, white for Easter, and so on) used that day.

ORIGINS OF THE CHURCH YEAR

Like many of the worship traditions in the Christian church, the church year has its origins in the liturgical observances of Judaism, particularly as they were practiced around the time of Jesus. Christians continued the Jewish pattern of daily and weekly prayer, but they structured their week around Sunday, which they called "the Lord's Day," the day of Jesus' resurrection and the outpouring of the Holy Spirit. In the Jewish calendar Sunday was known as the first day of the week, or sometimes the Eighth Day, symbolizing the fulfillment of time, the New Age. It was the day of creation, the day of light, and Christians adopted it as their primary occasion of celebration, rather than the Jewish Sabbath, the day of rest.

Very early in the church's history Christians began gathering every Sunday to celebrate the Eucharist as a ritual meal of bread and wine in which the risen Christ was known to them in the breaking of the bread and sharing of the cup. But soon the need arose for the teaching and formation of converts to the Christian faith, and the seasons and holy days of the church year developed in response to that need. Christian educator Joseph P. Russell has called the church year "the first curriculum of the church,"[61] a way of teaching the faith to those preparing for baptism in a lengthy process of formation that became known as the catechumenate.

The traditions and practices surrounding baptism were thus the kernel around which all other aspects of the church year developed. From the rites associated with Easter, baptisms developed the traditional celebrations of the Great Fifty Days of Easter and the season of preparation before Easter we call Lent. Over time, the fasting, study, prayers, and liturgies that marked the baptismal candidates' preparation for and celebration of Easter became part of the Lent-Easter-Pentecost cycle of the Christian year. The calendar dates for this cycle of the church year move each year, since the date for Easter depends on the cycle of the full moon, as does the feast of Passover. Some time later in the church's life, another cycle of feasts and fasts developed around the celebration of the birth of Christ. The dates for this Advent-Christmas-Epiphany cycle are fixed around the celebration of Christmas on December 25.

The fourth century was a particularly important time for the development of the church year as we know it today, as churches in the Holy Land developed liturgies to mark the days of Holy Week and Easter at the various sites at which Jesus suffered, died, and rose again. Pilgrims began to travel to Jerusalem to participate in these liturgies, and brought the traditions back to other countries as they returned. We have the diary of one such pilgrim, Egeria, a nun who visited Jerusalem in the year 385 and kept a diary to share with her sisters. She describes in great detail how the Jerusalem church marked the days of Lent, Holy Week, and Easter with a series of liturgies intentionally historical in their tone and content. The services she attended are remarkably familiar to us today.

Also during the first centuries of the church's life, the calendar of saints' days was evolving during the eras of persecution, in response to the growing need to commemorate the death of a Christian who died in witness to the faith. These martyrs were remembered both to honor their memory and to strengthen those who would soon be called upon to meet a similar fate. At first these commemorations were probably for local witnesses to the faith, but as the church grew, the practice of remembering and celebrating the saints and martyrs became more widespread, especially in the Middle Ages. You can find the biographies of the saints commemorated in the Episcopal Church in a book called *Lesser Feasts and Fasts*, which is updated every three years as new saints are added at our General Convention. It also provides Scripture readings and prayers to mark their feast days.

THE CHURCH CALENDAR

The section in the prayer book called The Calendar of the Church Year lists the days we mark as special occasions in the Episcopal Church. Sunday is the primary day of worship for Christians, as the "weekly remembrance of the glorious resurrection" of Christ (BCP 98). In addition, the calendar identifies a number of Principal Feasts, Holy Days, Days of Special Devotion, and Days of

Optional Observance. Many of these feasts and holy days have to do with the life of Jesus, including his conception, birth, baptism, transfiguration, passion, death, resurrection, and ascension. Other feasts in the church year focus on the church community, such as the coming of the Holy Spirit at Pentecost or the communion of believers throughout all time at All Saints' Day. The calendar also lists the saints whose lives and witness to the faith we commemorate.

Much of the calendar is concerned with what to do when feasts or fasts fall on the same day or on a Sunday, given the movable date of Easter, with all its associated feasts and fasts, that exists alongside the fixed calendar of saints' and holy days. Which day should take precedence? Since "all Sundays of the year are feasts of our Lord Jesus Christ" (BCP 16), the Sunday Eucharist is always primary, though a number of feasts may also be celebrated in conjunction with the Eucharist. The celebrations identified as "Principal Feasts" take precedence over any other holy day when there is overlap: these are Easter Day, Ascension Day, the Day of Pentecost, Trinity Sunday, All Saints' Day, Christmas Day, and the Epiphany. The Holy Name, the Presentation, and the Transfiguration may also be celebrated on a Sunday if they fall on that day in a given year.

Other holy days in the church year are identified as "major" or "minor" based on the closeness of their association with Jesus' life, death, and resurrection, and their basis in Scripture. You will sometimes hear the major feasts called "red letter days," from the old custom of printing church calendars in two colors: red for major feasts and black for lesser feasts. A major feast, for example, would be the Transfiguration—the day on which we remember Jesus' transfiguration on the mountain with some of his disciples, celebrated on August 6. The minor (or lesser) feasts include the days of commemorating the saints throughout the ages, such as Catherine of Siena on April 29 or Benedict of Nursia on July 11. When major or minor feasts happen to fall on a Sunday, however, the Sunday celebration of the Eucharist always takes precedence and the celebration of the feast is moved, or transferred, to the next closest available day.

The section in the prayer book outlining the calendar of the church year can seem like a maze of directions and rules. But when the church year is embodied in the life of a congregation, it becomes a fascinating, profoundly enriching way of discovering the Christian faith. The liturgies and traditions of the church year—from Advent lessons and carols through Christmas midnight mass to Epiphany processions with the wise men to the crèche, and from the start of Lent on Ash Wednesday to the pilgrimage through Holy Week to the celebrations of Easter and Pentecost—provide not just the basis for our education and remembrance of past events, but the means for our participation in the mysterious and ongoing redemption of the world. Again in the words of Massey Shepherd:

The Christian Year . . . makes present to us here and now all that is final and ultimate. The liturgy is not a discipline that prepares us step by step for some future goal and reward. The liturgy is at any time and in any place that goal present and real *now*.[62]

PROPER LITURGIES FOR SPECIAL DAYS

The section in the 1979 Book of Common Prayer called Proper Liturgies for Special Days contains the liturgies for six of the services for Lent, Holy Week, and Easter. The celebration of these liturgies is a relatively recent recovery in the Episcopal Church's life. Previous prayer books contained only additional prayers here and there to mark these occasions, since most of the medieval church's special rites for Lent, Holy Week, and Easter were prohibited by the first Anglican prayer books and the American prayer books largely followed their example. It was not until 1960 that an edition of the *Book of Offices* published by the Standing Liturgical Commission offered liturgies for these days, and the 1979 prayer book substantially expanded the recovery of these early liturgies. They are now widely kept throughout the Episcopal Church.

Ash Wednesday

With the Ash Wednesday liturgy we begin the season of Lent. It is a period of sober reflection, of repentance or turning away from patterns and actions that separate us from God, and of taking on disciplines that renew our spirits in preparation for Easter. This liturgy originates with the practice in the early church of excommunicating those whose serious and notorious sins caused great scandal. These individuals would be reinstated at the Easter Vigil following a period of penitence, including fasting and the wearing of sackcloth and ashes. Lent first began on the Monday following the first Sunday in Lent, but it was moved back to Wednesday sometime in the sixth century so that the season would have forty weekdays. By the ninth century this beginning to Lent became known as Ash Wednesday, and over time the discipline of public confession and the wearing of ashes was extended to all Christians.

The focus of Ash Wednesday is on penitence, or sorrow for sin, and fasting; the imposition of ashes is the physical embodiment of these themes, a reminder that we are mortal and that we receive eternal life as a free gift of God. At the appropriate time in the service you will be asked to come forward, and either stand or kneel. When the priest, deacon, or lay minister makes the sign of the cross with ashes on your forehead, he or she will say these words: "Remember that you are dust, and to dust you shall return." Sobering words, indeed. None of us likes to think about our own death or the deaths of those we love. And yet when we arc faced with the uncomfortable reality of human mortality, if our faith is to have any meaning, it is crucial that it can encompass even suffering and death, and thus be capable of seeing us through the passage to eternal life. Although on Ash Wednesday we are contemplating our mortality, we are also offering grateful thanks for our salvation in Jesus Christ, remembering that "it is only by [God's] gracious gift that we are given everlasting life" (BCP 265).

Palm Sunday

The full name given in the 1979 prayer book for this day is The Sunday of the Passion: Palm Sunday. These two traditional names reveal the dual focus of this day: Jesus' suffering and death on the Friday of Passover, and his triumphal entry into Jerusalem only a few days before. The liturgy as we have it now is a combination of several ancient rites that would have been done over the course of a number of hours.

The service begins with the Liturgy of the Palms, usually held somewhere other than the normal worship space to provide the congregation a path for the procession with palms. After a prayer the deacon reads one of the gospel passages describing Jesus' entry into Jerusalem riding on a donkey as the people "cut branches from the trees and spread them on the road" (Matt 21:8).

After the reading of the gospel, the priest or bishop will bless the palm branches to be used in the procession. Most congregations today use the palm fronds available from church supply houses, but the prayer book actually encourages the earlier custom of using the freshly cut branches of local trees and shrubs, even supplemented by flowers. As the scholar Dom Gregory Dix wryly notes, the single strands of palm fronds we have now, like the small crosses many congregations like to fold them into, "can hardly be waved and certainly fail to signify a parade."[63] Still, the symbolism is there, even though in a mild form.

After the deacon dismisses the people, the procession begins, led by the crucifer, acolytes, altar party, and choir, into the church's worship space. After the procession, the tone and focus of the service changes distinctly, from the triumphal entry to the approaching death of Jesus on the cross. This is the shift from the "parade" of the palms in joyful celebration to the sorrowful remembrance of Jesus' passion. The palm fronds are put away, and we listen to the readings from Scripture for the Sunday of the Passion, including the passion gospel.

The passion gospel for Palm Sunday is an extended reading from Matthew, Mark, or Luke (John is read on Good Friday) that tells the story of Jesus' prayer in the garden of Gethsemane, his trial and torture at the hands of the Romans, his crucifixion and death on the cross, and his burial in the tomb of Joseph of Arimathea. It can be read or chanted in a number of ways, though among the most common today is as a dramatic reading, involving a narrator and several people from the congregation who are given various speaking parts.

Following the reading of the passion gospel, the service continues as a normal though solemn Sunday Eucharist. Holy Week has begun.

Maundy Thursday

In the early church it became the practice to celebrate a "Supper of the Lord" on the Thursday evening of Holy Week, and by the seventh century this service was called Maundy Thursday, from the word *mandatum,* or commandment. The Eucharist is the central focus for this celebration of the institution of the Lord's Supper and the honoring of Jesus' commandment to "love one another as I have loved you," often symbolized by the washing of one another's feet. So the liturgy for Maundy Thursday in this section of the prayer book is more of a simple outline, providing a collect and the lectionary readings for the service, and an anthem to be sung or said at the footwashing. Additional prayers and directions for the footwashing can be found in *The Book of Occasional Services.*

Good Friday

During the first centuries of the church, Good Friday, Holy Saturday, and the Easter Vigil were all one single feast commemorating both the death and resurrection of Jesus. By the time Egeria went on pilgrimage to the Holy Land in the fourth century, however, a number of special liturgies had been developed to mark each of these days. These Holy Week rites, prayers, and ceremonies spread widely during the Middle Ages, were curtailed at the Reformation, and have now been adapted and restored in the 1979 prayer book.

The passion gospel is read on Good Friday as on Palm Sunday, again often as a dramatic presentation, but today's reading is from John, following the tradition of the oldest lectionaries and Anglican prayer books. Especially on this day, the passion gospel is the heart of the liturgy, as we recall the suffering and death of Jesus on the cross for the salvation of the world.

The Solemn Collects are likewise distinctive on this day. In this ancient form of prayer, the deacon or other leader bids the prayers of the congregation for the church, for "all nations and peoples of the earth, and for those in authority among them," for those who suffer, and for those who "have not received the Gospel of Christ" (BCP 279). The celebrant then allows time for silent prayer before concluding each bidding with a collect. Liturgical scholars believe this is the form used in Rome for the prayers of the people from the third or fourth century until those prayers were no longer included in the eucharistic liturgy. The biddings included in the 1979 prayer book date to the fourth or perhaps the third century; the collects are from the fifth. They are well worth praying on other days of the year, in our daily devotions or in small gatherings of Christians at prayer.

The option of offering devotions before the cross, sometimes called the Veneration of the Cross, is restored in this prayer book and may follow the Solemn Collects. Three anthems recovered from medieval missals and books of hours are provided. These anthems offer praise and adoration for the work of Christ on the cross:

> We glory in your cross, O Lord,
> *and praise and glorify your holy resurrection;*
> *for by virtue of your cross*
> *joy has come to the whole world.* (BCP 281)

One or more of these anthems may be sung or said while those who so desire go forward to kneel before, touch, or kiss a wooden cross brought into the church for that purpose. This form of honoring the cross of Christ is meaningful for many Episcopalians and distasteful for others. Such devotion is never required, but is offered for those who wish to express their gratitude in a tangible way. The sixth-century hymn "Sing, my tongue, the glorious battle," or another hymn "extolling the glory of the cross" (BCP 282), may follow the reading or singing of the anthems.

Some congregations choose to conclude the Good Friday service at this point with the Lord's Prayer and the concluding prayer, while others follow the tradition of receiving communion from the reserved sacrament. Good Friday and Holy Saturday are the only days in the church year on which the Eucharist may not be celebrated, as part of the fast before Easter. On Good Friday we receive the bread and wine consecrated on Maundy Thursday the night before. The liturgical scholar Marion J. Hatchett notes that "early sacramentaries make clear that on this day the reserved Sacrament in both kinds was brought to the altar in a simple manner" and, in contrast to the abundance of prayers and hymns that usually accompany communion, on Good Friday it was "administered in silence."[64]

Holy Saturday

Again on Holy Saturday there is no celebration of the Eucharist. In the early church this was a day of fasting before the Easter Vigil begun in the evening. Anglican prayer books have long provided a simple liturgy with prayers and readings from Scripture for this day, and the 1979 prayer book follows this custom. This is a day of rest and reflection, recalling Jesus' body lying in the tomb after the terrors of Friday. There are few traditions for keeping this day other than this simple office, but in one congregation to which I belonged many years ago it was their custom to work in the soil on Holy Saturday, gathering as a community to garden and tend the grounds of the church. This is a day for being grounded in the *humus*, the word from which we derive "humility"; it is a day for staying close to the earth from which we came and to which our bodies will one day return.

Easter Vigil

Easter is probably the earliest annual feast celebrated by the church, and is rooted in the Jewish Passover feast celebrating the exodus from Egypt and entrance into the Promised Land. For the early Christians, Jesus' death and resurrection were the fulfillment of this feast, and they used the same word for the Jewish Passover and the Christian Easter: *pascha*. By the time of Hippolytus, writing about 215, the early church was keeping a vigil on Saturday night before the celebration of Easter baptisms at dawn on Sunday. The blessing of the new fire and the singing of a theological hymn called the *Exsultet* was added soon after, as was the tradition of reading a number of lessons from the Old and New Testaments. The vigil remained the principal occasion for baptisms until the early Middle Ages, when the baptism of infants became the norm.

Since the vigil is newly restored in the 1979 prayer book, keeping the ancient Great Vigil of Easter is a new tradition in many Episcopal parishes. However, liturgically speaking it is the foundation for the rest of the seasons and liturgies of the church year. In Marion Hatchett's view, "Other baptisms of the year reflect this primary baptismal rite. Other Eucharists of the year are, to use the analogy of Augustine of Hippo, the repeatable part of this rite."[65] In other words, what we do on this night is a defining moment for

Christians each year, recalling our identity as followers of the Christ and our faith in the redemptive action of God. What we do the rest of the year, including the celebration of Sunday Eucharists, flows from this fundamental rite.

There are a number of elements in the Easter Vigil that are unique; others are quite familiar but have added significance in this remarkable setting. The vigil is held in darkness, usually in the evening on Saturday but possibly in the predawn hours of Sunday morning. It begins with the Service of Light, in which we light the new fire and the paschal candle. Legend has it that Saint Patrick knew of the lighting of the new fire, and this tradition may well be Celtic in origin. The paschal candle, a very large white taper carried by the deacon, is lit from the flame of the new fire. From this candle the hand-held candles of the congregation are then lit. The paschal candle will be lit at every service, if not continuously, until the feast of Pentecost.

The deacon then chants the *Exsultet*, an ancient blessing of the paschal candle that calls upon the entire company of heaven and earth to praise and worship the God who has redeemed the world through the victory of Christ over death. We are reminded that on this holy night of Easter eve, as at the first Easter, "all who believe in Christ are delivered from the gloom of sin, and are restored to grace and holiness of life." Indeed, it is on this night that "earth and heaven are joined and man is reconciled to God" (BCP 287). The *Exsultet* is a profoundly moving statement of our faith.

The Liturgy of the Word then follows, in which we hear readings from Scripture. The number of readings is left to the discretion of the congregation, but at least two must be read, and usually four or five or more, since a substantial number of readings is basic to any vigil. The readings focus on "the record of God's saving deeds in history" (BCP 288), and are interspersed with psalms and canticles.

After the readings we celebrate Easter baptisms, as was the custom in the early church. If there are no candidates in a congregation in a given year, the renewal of baptismal vows is done instead, as we reaffirm our renunciation of evil and our commitment to Jesus Christ.

Finally, we celebrate the Holy Eucharist. It is usually at this point that the lights in the church are turned on, the candles on the altar are lit, and the organ or piano leads the congregation in a joyous singing of the *Gloria in excelsis* or another song of praise. People often bring bells or play trumpets or tambourines in accompaniment, helping to "make a joyful noise before the Lord." As we hear once again the familiar words of the gospel, the creed, and the eucharistic prayer, they can be filled with fresh significance in this new dawn after the long weeks of Lent. We then share our Easter communion within the body of Christ, participating in the very life of the God "who made this most holy night to shine with the glory of the Lord's resurrection" (BCP 295).

QUESTIONS FOR REFLECTION AND DISCUSSION

1. What holiday traditions do you remember keeping in your childhood? What celebrations or commemorations do you keep in your family today? What meaning do these traditions have in your family? In what ways are the liturgical services of the church involved in these traditions, if at all?

2. What liturgies in the church that mark feasts or seasons in the church year have you attended, or are particularly memorable to you? What were your lasting impressions? How was your faith changed by them? What did they teach you about the Christian faith?

3. Read the *Exsultet* (BCP 286–87). What phrases or images stand out to you? Which words have particular meaning? Which are confusing or strange?

Making Vows
Confirmation, Marriage, and Ordination

In the name of God, I take you to be my wife, to have and to hold from this day forward, for better for worse, for richer for poorer, in sickness and in health, to love and to cherish, until we are parted by death. This is my solemn vow.

(BCP 427)

The church is fragrant with the scent of the white flowers surrounding the altar and adorning the end of each pew. The abundant candlelight gives a soft, warm glow to the faces turned toward the two people in the center, as they exchange their rings and make their promises of love and faithfulness to each other. It is a sacred, solemn, deeply joyous moment. It is also a moment when those who stand near to witness these vows reflect on the vows they have made in their own lives.

The priest standing between the couple recalls the day she made her ordination vows almost a decade ago, when she promised to "endeavor so to minister the Word of God and the sacraments of the New Covenant, that the reconciling love of Christ may be known and received" (BCP 532). How well has she lived in accordance with those vows, she wonders. They have affected the way she lives each day, the work she does, the priorities she makes, the people who form her community. What joy—and heartache—her work in the church has brought her! How could she be more faithful to those vows in the future?

The bride's younger sister, standing among the other beautifully dressed women in the bride's party, anticipates her confirmation the next Sunday when the bishop visits. She has been preparing for that moment for weeks, attending classes and trying to keep a rule of life that includes daily prayer and Bible study. The discussion in the classes has awakened all sorts of questions and hopes in her, as well as a desire to know God, to have a sense of meaning and purpose in her life that is larger than her own happiness. But is she ready? she wonders. Will she be able to keep her vow to renew her commitment to Jesus Christ and to "follow him as my Savior and Lord" (BCP 415)? What does that mean, exactly? How is she called to live the gospel today, at her school and among her community of family and friends?

Sitting on the other side of the aisle in the front pew, the groom's mother searches for a tissue in her purse. Her eyes have filled with tears at the sight of her son exchanging the same vows she had said so many years ago. He has the same determination, the same overwhelming love shining in his eyes, the same optimism and hope she remembered so well. Why did her marriage fail? she wonders sadly. How could they have kept their love alive, instead of drifting so far apart over the years of child rearing and work? Her parents just celebrated their fiftieth wedding anniversary last year, their lives now so deeply and lovingly intertwined they seem inseparable. What kept them growing together through all those years of joy and heartache, of good times and bad? And how does she come to terms with the failure of the vows she made with holy intention before God and the Christian community, vows that were dissolved in the cold isolation of a lawyer's office years later? How can she help her son to live out the vows he is making this day with the same holy intention?

THE MAKING OF COVENANTS

We are shaped by the commitments we make in our lives. Some of these commitments are relatively minor: we agree to meet for coffee tomorrow afternoon, or to produce a document by next week. Other commitments are foundational to our lives, determining who will be our family, where we will live, the work we will undertake, what will be our religious convictions. These commitments are often called covenants: solemn promises we make to God and to one another in the presence of God. Covenants form the frameworks within which we live our lives, and they are different from simple commitments in that God is an integral part of the covenantal relationship.

Covenants focus our lives in a particular way through the choices they require us to make among the many possibilities available to us. They enable us to say: of all the people I could marry I choose *you*, of all the vocations or careers I could choose I will do *this*, of all the religions in the world I embrace *this* one. We promise to love someone while "forsaking all others," to focus our energy on becoming skilled in a particular vocation, to participate in the life of a single faith community. Our covenants thus limit our options, in a sense, forcing us to choose which path we will take among all the many good and honorable paths that are open to us, and thus freeing us to embrace that path wholeheartedly, with a single focus.

Covenants also give us the time we need to deepen our love, to develop our knowledge, to practice our faith. When we promise to love "till death do us part" or to be an active participant in a particular faith community, we are committing ourselves to make it through the rocky places, the hard patches, the times of confusion and doubt. It is often far easier to live without such commitments, to follow our whims, to enjoy relationships only while they "feel good": when they become tedious or difficult or demanding we can then say goodbye and move on. And yet skimming along the surface rarely suffices for long, and most of us begin to yearn for more substance in our lives. By giving us the time and stability to grow and develop, our covenants thus encourage us to love more deeply, to do our work with greater skill, to live our faith with a fuller awareness of what we believe, all the while held and encouraged by the steadfast and energetic support of God.

While we recognize the importance of stable commitments in the structuring of our lives, we must also realize that covenants can change over time. Even the covenants God has made with the human race have changed in the way they are expressed in succeeding generations.

The fundamental commitment of the unconditional love of the Creator has remained constant, but that love has been expressed in various covenants. In the book of Genesis we read of God's promise to Noah never to destroy life on earth again through the waters of a flood. Then God gives Noah a "sign of the covenant": a rainbow in the sky. "When the bow is in the clouds," God tells Noah, "I will see it and remember the everlasting covenant between God and every living creature of all flesh that is on the earth" (Gen 9:16).

Later, in his covenant with Abraham, God promises to make of Abraham "a great nation" and to make his descendants as numerous as all the stars in the heaven. Abraham will be "the ancestor of a multitude of nations," and God makes an "everlasting covenant, to be God to you and your offspring after you," giving them all the land of Canaan forever (Gen 17:7–8). After the Exodus from slavery in Egypt, the celebration of the Passover and the practice of the law of Moses became essential ways of keeping the covenant with God. But this "Old Testament," or "Old Covenant," was seen by the followers of Jesus as fulfilled in a New Covenant made through the death and resurrection of the Messiah of God.

In much the same way, the covenants we make in our lives can change over time, because people and circumstances change. Some of the covenants we make are intended to be lifelong and thus are usually made only once, such as the vows we make at our baptism, confirmation, marriage, and ordination. In the church we number these four occasions of making vows before God sacraments, since they are intended to be tangible and visible signs of spiritual and invisible grace. At the same time, while these covenants are lifelong, they are also intended to be life giving, and when they stifle the very life they are intended to give they must be reconsidered and perhaps re-visioned. Sometimes, after much reflection and prayer, we are able with a whole heart to renew the covenants we made years ago; at other times we find we must end them with regret as well as with thanksgiving for the life they gave for a time.

A person ordained in one denomination, for example, may find he or she has so changed over the years that it is no longer possible to affirm wholeheartedly the beliefs or practices of that denomination. The person becomes so at odds with the practices of that church that his or her faith founders. If this dissonance and sense of constriction continues, it may be wise to consider ministry in a different denomination so the person's faith may continue to grow and deepen. Marriages too often reach moments of crisis, sometimes repeatedly, when the couple must decide whether to try to restructure their commitment and renew their covenant, or to part ways. Sometimes it is difficult to discern when to remain steadfast within a commitment that has grown stale or stifling but that still has the potential for life and love, and when it is destructive for everyone involved to maintain the structure of those vows when the love that inspired them has died.

CONFIRMATION

The promises we make at baptism—or those made on our behalf—are usually the first vows we make in our Christian journey. Closely connected with those baptismal vows to follow Christ as our Lord and Savior are the promises we make in the sacrament of confirmation. Episcopalians today usually encounter this rite either when joining the Episcopal Church from another denomination or when their children become teenagers or young adults and are ready to assume mature responsibility for their own faith. The purpose of confirmation as presented in the 1979 Book of Common Prayer is to provide an opportunity for those who were baptized as infants or young children to "make a mature public affirmation of their faith and commitment to the responsibilities of their Baptism and to receive the laying on of hands by the bishop" (BCP 412). This rite is also intended for those who were baptized as adults in another denomination but who have not been confirmed by a bishop, as a representative of the universal and apostolic church throughout the ages.

This intended purpose may seem simple and straightforward, but the liturgical roots of this sacrament are extraordinarily confusing and have been the source of much disagreement. The confusion lies in the history of confirmation. The primary elements of the rite— mature public affirmation of faith and the laying on of hands by a bishop of the church—were originally part of the baptismal liturgy in the early church, when the church was small enough for bishops to be the leaders of every congregation and adult baptism was the norm. Over time, however, presbyters or priests were placed as the bishop's representatives in the larger congregations, and the prevalence of infant baptism precluded any public affirmation of faith or formation in Christian teaching.

So these two elements of the baptismal rite were separated from the service of baptism and performed later, when the bishop was present and the child was older, and confirmation was thus generally viewed as a completion of baptism. Even then, there was ongoing disagreement as to what age was appropriate for confirmation. In the thirteenth century alone these ages ranged from one to three to seven; a century later twelve was more common. Apparently confirmation was not seen as a high priority for many people in the pews, and as a way of encouraging its importance, in 1281 one archbishop decreed that no one could be admitted to communion without being confirmed, thus establishing a custom of linking the reception of communion with confirmation.

At the Reformation the picture regarding confirmation remains murky, with the various reformed traditions adopting different perspectives about its relationship to baptism. One of the fundamental questions asked about the sacrament of confirmation was: What actually happens? Do Christians who are baptized really need it? Since New Testament times, the giving of the Holy Spirit has been associated with baptism, and in the early and medieval church it was commonly held that in the baptismal liturgy during the prayer of the bishop, with the laying on of hands, the Holy Spirit came to dwell within the believer. At the time of the Reformation, then, the question arose of whether confirmation was the necessary completion of baptism with the gift of the Holy Spirit, or simply the adult reaffirmation of baptismal vows and the strengthening of the presence of that Spirit. Today we tend to agree with the second response, viewing baptism as the complete sacrament of initiation that includes the gift of the indwelling Holy Spirit, and confirmation as the reaffirmation of the vows made at baptism and a strengthening of the life of the Spirit within, helping believers live out those vows more fully.

One clear connection widely made at the Reformation that has continued in our present day is the link between confirmation and a period of formation and teaching in the Christian faith. In most Protestant churches of the time, including the Anglican Church, this meant being able to recite the Lord's Prayer, the articles of faith, and the Ten Commandments, as well as to answer questions on the content of the catechism. The 1549 Book of Common Prayer went so far as to provide an introductory section within the confirmation rite that included teachings on the creed, the Lord's Prayer, the Ten Commandments, the catechism, and the meaning of baptism.

In the 1979 prayer book the continuing link between catechesis and confirmation is clear in the recommendation that the sacrament be offered to people "when they are ready and have been duly prepared" (BCP 412). Today this preparation often takes place in the form of confirmation or inquirers' classes, led by the clergy or teachers in the congregation and covering the basics of the Christian faith as it is lived in the Episcopal Church—Bible, prayer book, sacraments and worship, church history, and so on. Many congregations now incorporate a popular program of adolescent formation in the faith called Journey to Adulthood into their preparations for confirmation during the teenage years.[66] In Journey to Adulthood young people in the sixth through twelfth grades explore their faith within the context of Bible study, prayer, rites of passage, and outreach activities.

The liturgy for confirmation appears in two places in the 1979 prayer book, within the service for Holy Baptism and again as a separate rite in the section called the Pastoral Offices. The liturgies are identical; the second is simply used when no one is being baptized and all of the candidates are to be confirmed or received into the Episcopal Church from another denomination that practices confirmation or are reaffirming their baptismal vows. After the candidates reaffirm their renunciation of evil and renew their baptismal commitment to Jesus Christ, the bishop prays over the candidates, asking God to "renew in these your servants the covenant you made with them at their Baptism" and to "send them forth in the power of that Spirit to perform the service you set before them" (BCP 418).

Each candidate then comes forward to kneel before the bishop, who is usually seated in front of the altar. For confirmation, the bishop lays his or her hands on the head of each person, and prays that the person will receive strength, empowerment for service, and the grace to continue in the Christian life and "daily increase in your Holy Spirit more and more, until he comes to your everlasting kingdom" (BCP 418). Those to be received are recognized as "a member of the one holy catholic and apostolic Church" and are received into "the fellowship of this Communion" (BCP 418). And for those who are reaffirming their baptismal vows, the bishop prays that the Holy Spirit "who has begun a good work in you" may continue to "direct and uphold you in the service of Christ and his kingdom" (BCP 419).

As with all the sacraments of the church, the way grace is experienced through confirmation will vary with every person, but for many of us confirmation remains a memorable event in our lives. I was confirmed in the Episcopal Church in college, and I still remember the incredible warmth and sense of powerful strength and grace conveyed by the bishop's hands on my head as he prayed over me. Our confirmation as teenagers or young adults may be the first time we stand before others and make public vows of any kind, so in that way it marks one of the transition points or rites of passage to mature adulthood. And among churches that practice infant baptism, it is also usually the first time we as Christians state publicly our faith in Jesus Christ as our Lord and Savior. We can worship among the crowd for years, but when it comes time to stand on our own and proclaim what we believe, our faith can be immeasurably strengthened. The vows we make at confirmation can be a steadying reminder of the indissoluble nature of God's covenant of grace made in our baptism during the inevitable times of doubt and unfaithfulness in the years to come.

MARRIAGE

For many people today, the marriage ceremony is their first—and sometimes only—encounter with the Episcopal Church. The service as we have it in the 1979 prayer book incorporates many modern concerns for equality and inclusivity while preserving the traditional language and images that give solemnity to the vows as well as a sense of participating in a longstanding custom of the human race. The marriage rite is thus in many ways a fitting introduction to the

Episcopal Church, as it seeks in all its worship and community life to adapt and change with the times while preserving what is essential and timeless in the church's tradition.

Nearly all human cultures have rituals and ceremonies associated with the joining of two people into a single family unit. The marriage customs we have received in the Book of Common Prayer have their roots in the Jewish, Greek, and Roman cultures in which the early church developed, though in some cases the meaning of the rituals has changed over time. In pagan Roman weddings, for example, the man placed a ring on the woman's fourth finger of her left hand as a sign of possession; today we tend to exchange rings as a sign of our love and fidelity to one another. After a banquet and procession to their house, the man carried the woman over the threshold of the door, where they lit the hearth fire together to symbolize their making of a new home; today many people have already made a home together even before the marriage, though the custom of carrying the woman over the threshold is still carried out by some, often with some amusement.

During the early Middle Ages the church in the West simply adapted many of the traditional Roman customs, substituting Christian prayers for the prayers to the Roman gods, and celebrating a Eucharist instead of offering the traditional pagan sacrifices. In a Roman wedding, for example, after the public ceremony of vows and celebration, the couple went to their new home, where a person representing Juno, the goddess of marriage and childbearing, prayed with them while preparing the marriage bed. The Christian liturgical books of the early Middle Ages likewise contain prayers for blessing the newlyweds in bed. American cultures today tend to shy away from the church's involvement in such intimacies, and the prayer book has included in the marriage ceremony itself tastefully subdued forms of prayers for the conception of children.

The 1549 prayer book gathered ceremonies and prayers from several Reformed and English traditions available at the time, and the rite in that book is quite similar to what we have today. One noticeable change is that marriages were to take place in the context of the Sunday Eucharist; when that custom gradually fell into disuse, the marriage ceremony was left as an abbreviated service with no readings from Scripture or celebration of the Eucharist. Weddings today tend to take place in separate services during the week, though in the 1979 prayer book the ceremony is once again placed in the context of a liturgy of the Word and sacrament. The Eucharist is encouraged but optional for those situations in which such a celebration would be awkward, or would be a painful sign of the disunity of the church for many members of the family whose faith traditions would not allow them to receive communion.

After the opening hymn or entrance music for the procession, the service begins with an exhortation that originated in the 1549 prayer book, with quotations from several sources, including the marriage rite of Martin Luther. It speaks of marriage as "Holy Matrimony," not simply a legal contract between two people. Christian marriage is a covenant "established by God in creation," and this bond is a sign of the mysterious union of Christ and the church. The exhortation goes on to list three reasons for the practice of marriage: mutual joy "in heart, body, and mind," help and comfort in good times and bad, and the procreation and nurture of children. It concludes with a concern to maintain the solemnity of this vow: "Therefore marriage is not to be entered into unadvisedly or lightly, but reverently, deliberately, and in accordance with the purposes for which it was instituted by God" (BCP 423).

The celebrant then asks the bride and groom whether they know of any reason or lawful impediment to the marriage. This question has become a dramatic moment in films or novels as a secret spouse or witness suddenly appears to stop the ceremony, but actually the question is posed in order to ease the annulment process when in fact one of the persons is already married but fails to acknowledge that previous relationship publicly.

The Declaration of Consent follows, in which the man and woman declare their intention to marry. In earlier centuries the declaration took place at some time before the marriage, much like the Jewish practice of betrothal. Today both the man and woman declare their intentions within the context of the service, though the custom of announcing the upcoming marriage during several services prior to the wedding—called publishing the banns of marriage—continues in many places. The 1979 prayer book allows for the option of the bride's parents or a friend "giving away" or presenting the bride, but since this custom originated in a time when women were considered the property of men, many people today choose not to incorporate this custom into their wedding ceremony. An alternative sentence of presentation is provided that includes both the man and the woman in the presentation. The celebrant asks, "Who presents this woman and this man to be married to each other?" and the couple's parents or other chosen individuals respond together (BCP 437).

After the collect, readings from Scripture, and homily or "other response to the Readings," the vows of marriage are exchanged. In Jewish, Greek, and Roman cultures the couple joined hands as a sign of their marriage, and this custom is followed in the 1979 prayer book when the man and woman join hands during the exchange of vows. Different cultural views of marriage can be seen in the various forms these vows have taken over the centuries: until the 1928 prayer book the woman's vow included a promise to "obey" her husband, for example, and in the earlier English Sarum tradition the woman likewise promised to "be gentle and obedient in the bed and at the table."[67] Today the vows of the man and woman are identical. It is worth noting here that at the moment they exchange vows, the man and the woman are the ministers of this sacrament. The clergyperson officiating at the service is simply there to ask the questions, pronounce the marriage the man and woman have made in the sight of God, and bless the marriage vows they have made.

After the man and woman exchange vows the priest or bishop may bless the rings exchanged or given as a symbol of the vows. The custom of exchanging rings dates from ancient Rome, when a man gave a ring of betrothal to a woman; by the ninth century another ring was then given at the time of the wedding. The blessing we have now speaks of the ring being a sign of honoring the other with "all that I am, and all that I have," echoing the original blessing in the 1549 prayer book: "with my body I thee worship; and with all my worldly goods I thee endow."

The celebrant then pronounces "that they are husband and wife," a custom brought into the Anglican prayer books from the Lutheran tradition. This part of the marriage service concludes with the sobering words of the intended permanence of these vows, "Those whom

God has joined together let no one put asunder," and the entire congregation responds, "Amen"—so be it, let it be so (BCP 428).

The prayers that follow are a blending of prayers from older prayer books and traditions and prayers newly composed for this prayer book. They include the now optional prayer for the "gift and heritage of children," as well as prayers that express the hopes and ideals of marriage as a way of "ordering their common life" with "wisdom and devotion" so that "each may be to the other a strength in need, a counselor in perplexity, a comfort in sorrow, and a companion in joy." The prayers also recognize that inevitably the couple will hurt each other, and asks God's grace to help them to "acknowledge their fault, and to seek each other's forgiveness." They conclude with a recognition that the marriage bond is intended to be the stable core of an ever-widening circle of care for family, friends, companions, and members of the community, and that the love the couple shares will enable them to "reach out in love and concern for others" (BCP 429).

Finally, just before the exchange of the peace and the celebration of the Eucharist, the bishop or priest blesses the couple as they kneel before him or her, asking God to "bless them in their work and in their companionship; in their sleeping and in their waking; in their joys and in their sorrows; in their life and in their death" (BCP 430). The blessing also makes it clear that marriage is a sacrament, a means of experiencing God's grace in this life and in the life to come, and not simply a state of two people living together:

> God the Father, God the Son, God the Holy Spirit, bless, preserve, and keep you; the Lord mercifully with his favor look upon you, and fill you with all spiritual benediction and grace; that you may faithfully live together in this life, and in the age to come have life everlasting. (BCP 431)

And yet despite the ideals so beautifully expressed in the prayers and blessings of the marriage rite, it must be acknowledged that in a culture in which divorce and second or third marriages are extremely common, the church has not always been a place of support for Christians in the midst of marital difficulties. Couples whose marriage vows have foundered and dissolved often find congregations are silent and distant, sometimes even rejecting, during a time when they desperately need help, comfort, and guidance. Some congregations are seeking to change that, and have developed liturgies that address the painful ending of marriage vows while still upholding the solemnity of the vows that were intended to be lifelong. In one congregation in Washington, D.C., for example, when renewal of the marriage bond is clearly not possible even after serious and long-term counseling, the couple may gather with their children, families, and friends in the church, where they give thanks to God for the good things that came to pass as a result of their life together. They then return their rings and release each other from their vows, praying that God will bless the other as he or she grows in grace in the years to come. Such a rite can bring healing and closure to a marriage that no longer has the potential for loving union, and can release the two people from vows that constrict God's grace, giving them the possibility for new life and continued growth in Christ within the church community.

In much the same way, many congregations seek to help individuals who are divorced who seek to marry again. In the Episcopal Church the process for remarriage requires discernment of the causes for the failure of the first marriage, as well as counseling that encourages repentance and an effort to change any unhealthy patterns of behavior that may create difficulties in the second marriage. Finally, remarriage requires the approval of the bishop as the representative of the wider church, who declares that the first marriage has indeed ended and the individual is free to marry again.

This process of remarriage may seem overly cumbersome or intrusive to those in a society in which divorce is a fact of life. It is nonetheless a way of affirming that, while acknowledging the reality of divorce, the church's marriage rite still seeks to uphold the ideal of lifelong commitment and loving union that mirrors the indissoluble union of Christ and the church. Such a commitment provides the foundation for stability and offers the couple the gift of time—rare commodities these days, in our fast-paced, mobile societies. In exchanging these vows the couple promises to give their love time to grow and change—to "abide" in love. We do not use the word "abide" much today, but Jesus used it a lot in the Gospel of John to talk about how God relates to us: "Abide in my love," Jesus urged his disciples, "just as I abide in God the Father's love." In the midst of our transitory world, the couple promises to abide, to give each other time to grow in their love, time to deepen their wonder and knowledge of each other, time to become the people they yearn to be.

No discussion of marriage today is complete without considering the question of lifelong commitments between people of the same gender. As some American states and cities move ahead with the granting of marriage licenses to same-sex couples while others seek to ban such marriages, the various churches are also asked to make decisions regarding the blessing of these unions. The controversy surrounding these relationships is intense and promises to remain so for some time, but the Episcopal Church has chosen to uphold the sanctity of marriage as between a man and a woman while leaving the option of blessing same-sex unions to the discretion of each diocese and parish. Since our 74th General Convention in 2003 approved a resolution that authorized dioceses to develop distinctive rites for the blessing of same-sex relationships (the marriage rite is intended for use between a man and woman only), a number of dioceses have begun to adapt and create liturgies for that purpose. Their experiences will then be brought back to the table for further discussion in future General Conventions.

ORDINATION

In many ways those preparing for ordination today undergo a formation process similar to the early church's catechumenate: a two- or three-year period of discernment, prayer, study, and growth in the Christian faith and life, culminating in a festive and solemn liturgical rite in which the candidate makes lifelong vows before the bishop to follow Christ and serve the church and world in his name. Indeed, many of the ceremonies associated with ordination, such as anointing with oil, were originally part of the early baptismal rites that were performed by or on behalf of the bishop. Like confirmation, ordination to Holy Orders is a function of the bishop that has never been delegated to the priests or deacons of the church, and thus is included in the prayer book's section called Episcopal

Services—services at which the bishop (*episcopos* in Greek), the person entrusted with the oversight (*episcope*) of a particular region of the church called a diocese, must preside.

During the second half of the twentieth century the church reconsidered its views and practice of ministry among the laity, the whole people of God. Not too many years ago the word "minister" in common parlance applied only to those who were ordained; today we are often reminded that we are *all* ministers of the church by virtue of our baptism. The catechism in the 1979 Book of Common Prayer makes it clear that the "ministers of the Church are lay persons, bishops, priests, and deacons" (BCP 855). Laypeople are increasingly visible and active participants and leaders in the ministries of the church in the world today, in their workplace, schools, homes, and communities. They are also integral leaders of the church's liturgies today, as well as the primary "movers and shakers" in much of the church's outreach, education, and pastoral ministries.

The role of the ordained is thus in many ways more sharply delineated today than it was when the clergy were expected to perform all the ministries of the church. The roles of bishops, priests, and deacons do not replace or usurp the roles of the laity; rather, they are intended to complement and support one another in a stable ordering of the wide variety of the church's ministries. Unlike the laity, the ordained tend to focus more of their energies on the ministries and liturgical needs of the institutional church rather than the wider community. As they have since New Testament times, bishops have responsibility for the oversight of the church, while deacons emphasize the service (*diakonia*) of the church that embodies the ongoing ministry of Christ in the world. The priesthood probably developed from the elders who functioned with various church communities, and became the designated leaders for the bishop as congregations grew beyond the size that one bishop could effectively lead. Thus priests (or presbyters) are an extension of the pastoral ministry of the bishop at the local level, often serving as the liturgical, pastoral, and administrative leaders of congregations.

In the course of the Middle Ages the organic and somewhat fluid nature of ministry in the early church, in which the necessary functions of church life were carried out by ordained and laypeople together, solidified into seven hierarchical orders of ordained ministry, with the episcopate and priesthood at the top. The reformers sought to return to an earlier view of ministry by reasserting the early church's practice of having bishops, priests, and deacons, though they continued to be viewed through the medieval lens of a stepladder to sacred power, from deacon to priest to bishop.

This hierarchical perspective has continued to inform the church's understanding of ordained ministries to our own day: the ordination rite of the 1928 prayer book, for example, offers a prayer that the newly ordained deacons "may so well behave themselves in this inferior Office, that they may be found worthy to be called unto the higher Ministries in thy Church" (1928 BCP, 535). Such hierarchical language has been removed in the 1979 prayer book, and as we continue to live into this restoration of the early church's view of distinct but equal ministries within the body of Christ, it is growing less common to encounter the medieval perspective. Many of us hope one day that the liturgical churches will move ahead with considering a restoration of ordination directly to the order to which a person is called, rather than retaining ordination to a transitional orders of ministry.

The restoration of the diaconate as a "full and equal order" rather than merely a transitional stop on the way to priesthood has played an important role in the renewal of the church's understanding of all the orders of ministry, including that of the laity. I remember a conversation I once had in seminary with a man preparing for ordination to the priesthood. He told me that living, working, studying, and praying alongside me as I prepared for ordination to the diaconate had clarified for him his unique call to the priesthood. We were doing much the same things—going to class, performing our work duties, studying in the library, praying in the chapel. But the way in which we did these common acts was informed by a different call, a distinct perspective and focus. His place of fulfillment was as a pastor and teacher, a mediator and presider at worship, while my natural mode of being and the source of a sense of meaning and purpose in my life was found in service to others, supporting and encouraging them in their own particular ministries within and beyond the church. Our vocations were distinct and complementary rather than on a ladder of ascending importance, and seeing those distinctions helped us both to value our own unique contributions to the life of the church.

In any consideration of ordained ministry, it is important to remember that the ordained are not the only ministers in the church. In their book *Liturgy for Living*, the liturgical scholars Louis Weil and Charles Price identify three "crucial dimensions" of the church's life that are embodied in the orders of bishops, priests, and deacons: responsibility, priesthood, and service. And yet having these three orders does not mean that those who are not ordained are any less involved in the church's ministry in and to the world. They eloquently note:

> The ordained ministry does not perform these functions on behalf of the church or instead of the church. Deacons do not serve so that other Christian people don't have to serve. Ordained deacons serve in order to *enable* the church to serve better. Priests do not mediate in order that other Christians can be relieved of their commission to represent God to the world and the world to God. Priests function to make the priesthood of all believers possible. Bishops are not responsible for the church so that the church as a whole does *not* need to be responsible for the rest of the world, but in order that every Christian, in the particular way open to him or her, may exercise the basic Christian ministry of responsible oversight.[68]

The ordained ministries of the church thus represent and enable the ministries of the entire people of God.

The liturgies for the ordination of bishops, priests, and deacons in the 1979 Book of Common Prayer are a blending of ancient rites from the early, medieval, and Reformation churches, earlier Anglican prayer books, and newly composed texts. The earliest text we have for ordination is in the third-century *Apostolic Tradition* of Hippolytus, which probably reflects the customs of the church in Rome at that time. Bishops, presbyters, and deacons were elected by the people of a local congregation and ordained on a Sunday by a bishop or group of bishops through prayer and the laying on of hands. The newly ordained person then performed the appropriate tasks and roles of that order of ministry in a celebration of the Eucharist. The bishop offered the eucharistic prayer; the presbyter joined other presbyters in standing by the bishop during the eucharistic prayer; and the deacon prepared the table and assisted in the distribution of communion.

During the Middle Ages the ordination rites became more elaborate and lengthy, with additional prayers and ceremonies adding to their solemnity. At the time of the Reformation, there was much debate among the reformers as to what forms of ordained ministry, if any, should be retained in the Protestant churches. Martin Luther and several other reformers believed that the essential elements of the ordination rite were prayer and the laying on of hands before a gathering of the church community, all in the context of the reading of Scripture. Their thinking strongly influenced the reformers in England, and many of their ideas, particularly those of the German theologian Martin Bucer, were included in the early Anglican prayer books. The ordination rites of the 1979 Book of Common Prayer contain many elements from the reformers' efforts, while seeking to restore the traditions and texts from the earlier rites as well.

The classic distinctions among bishops, priests, and deacons are made clear in the ordination rites themselves, especially in the section called The Examination, which also contains a series of questions to the ordinand. Bishops are "called to be one with the apostles," proclaiming and interpreting the gospel while guarding "the faith, unity, and discipline of the Church." They are to celebrate and "provide for the administration" of the church's sacraments. Bishops are to ordain priests and deacons, and to share in the ordination of other bishops. They are "to be in all things a faithful pastor and wholesome example for the entire flock of Christ." Along with other bishops, the newly ordained bishop will "share in the leadership of the Church throughout the world." They are the "chief priest and pastor" in the diocese, called to "encourage and support all baptized people in their gifts and ministries" (BCP 517–18).

Priests are called to the work of "pastor, priest, and teacher," proclaiming the gospel and serving others in love. They are to "preach, to declare God's forgiveness to penitent sinners, to pronounce God's blessing," and to celebrate the sacraments. In all things, priests are expected to be guided by the counsel of the bishop, to "persevere in prayer," and "so to minister the Word of God and the sacraments of the New Covenant, that the reconciling love of Christ may be known and received" (BCP 531–32).

The examination for the deacon notes that "every Christian is called to follow Jesus Christ, serving God the Father, through the power of the Holy Spirit." But the deacon is called to a "special ministry of servanthood" directly under the bishop, serving all people and especially "the poor, the weak, the sick, and the lonely." Deacons are to "make Christ and his redemptive love known," interpreting to the church "the needs, concerns, and hopes of the world." They also assist the bishops and priests in public worship and the administration of the sacraments. At all times, they are "to show Christ's people that in serving the helpless they are serving Christ himself" (BCP 543).

One of the most memorable moments in many ordination services is the ancient practice of having a period of silent prayer following the singing or chanting of the *Veni Creator Spiritus* or *Veni Sancte Spiritus*, ancient hymns asking that the Holy Spirit be present among the gathered community. "Come, Holy Ghost, our souls inspire, and lighten with celestial fire," we sing quietly. "Thou the anointing Spirit art, who dost thy sevenfold gifts impart," we pray as the clergy (and in some places, laypeople as well) form a close circle around the kneeling ordinand. The bishop then lays his or her hands on the ordinand's head, and those gathered around likewise lay hands on the ordinand or on each other's shoulders as an expression of our mutual sharing of ministries within the church. It is an intense moment of holy intention and the fulfillment of the deepest hopes for many ordinands. Like the moment in which vows are exchanged in the marriage ceremony, this culmination of the ordination rite often evokes powerful memories, yearnings, and prayers of thanksgiving among those gathered in prayer for the varied and abundant gifts of ministry shared in the Body of Christ.

For the newly ordained, the making of public vows before God and in the presence of the gathered community is a life-changing event, just as marriage and confirmation are. The church marks all of these occasions with prayer and the laying on of hands, whether it be the hands of the couple joined in marriage or the hands of the bishop on the heads of confirmands or ordinands. They are the moments in which we stand and declare our intentions, our loves, our beliefs, our hopes, our dreams. The covenants we make at these moments will shape who we are and how we live our lives. They can thus be a time of anxiety as well as of joy, and yet the words spoken to ordinands apply to us all as we seek to fulfill the vows we make: "May the Lord who has given you the will to do these things give you the grace and power to perform them. *Amen*" (BCP 532).

QUESTIONS FOR REFLECTION AND DISCUSSION

1. What vows have you made in your life? How well have you kept them? What or who helped you sustain and nurture your vows over the years?

2. In what ways has the church been a part of the vows you have made? How has the church provided help in the keeping of those vows? How could the church have been more helpful?

3. If you have made vows that could not endure the test of time, what encouraged you to end the covenant you made? Was the church part of that ending? How has the ending of the vow affected your life? Your faith?

Praying in the Midst of Life
The Pastoral Offices

*Into your hands, O merciful Savior, we commend your servant.
Acknowledge, we humbly beseech you, a sheep of your own fold, a
lamb of your own flock, a sinner of your own redeeming. Receive
her into the arms of your mercy, into the blessed rest of everlasting
peace, and into the glorious company of the saints in light. Amen.*

(BCP 499)

He sat very still, one hand holding a damp handkerchief, the other
clasped in the hand of his eldest daughter sitting beside him as the
priest was praying the prayer of commendation, gathered with the
other ministers around the coffin containing the body of his beloved
wife. The burial service is almost over, he thought. It would soon be
time to say a final goodbye to the body of the woman he had married over forty years ago.

His mind wandered back over the past months of her painfully
long illness, remembering all the visits the priest and parishioners
had made to their home, bringing the solace and strength of companionship, prayer, and Holy Communion in the midst of so much
sadness and loss. As he thought of how many funerals of friends and
loved ones he had attended in that very church over the years, his
eyes focused on the beautiful white pall covering the coffin, and he
noticed its carefully repaired edges were frayed from years of use. Its

heavy linen was stained from the repeated sprinkling with blessed water—just as her baptismal gown had been dampened by the waters of her baptism sixty-six years ago.

The tattered yet stately pall reminded him that even in the midst of his sudden loneliness he was not alone: he and his wife were still part of this same communion of saints on heaven and earth, though she was now in that place "where sorrow and pain are no more, neither sighing, but life everlasting." And he knew that it was this awareness of their eternal life in God that would see him through the days and weeks and years to come, until he too would cross over into that "glorious company of the saints in light" (BCP 499).

THE PASTORAL OFFICES

The 1979 Book of Common Prayer groups a number of liturgical rites together in a section called the Pastoral Offices. These liturgies focus on particular occasions in the lives of individual Christians, though most are not solitary rites but are intended to be celebrated in the context of a community Eucharist, or Morning or Evening Prayer. They are "pastoral" in the sense that they have to do with the care and nurture of people within the church, and a "pastor" or priest participates in them. We have already considered the pastoral offices of marriage and confirmation elsewhere in this book, but here we will look at the most commonly experienced of these rites marking important moments in our lives, from the birth of a child to significant turning points of repentance and reconciliation to the loss of our loved ones through death.

A THANKSGIVING FOR THE BIRTH OR ADOPTION OF A CHILD

The birth or adoption of a child is a life-changing human experience many people share, one that can bring a powerful awareness of the mystery of life and of God's mercy and grace. For many Christian parents the first opportunity to offer thanks for this unspeakable gift is at the child's baptism, several weeks, months, or even years after the birth.

This empty space between the birth and the occasion of giving thanks was certainly my experience with our first child. When

Benjamin was born, we were filled with overwhelming gratitude for his safe arrival after days of difficult labor. We shared this joy with family and friends, many of them fellow members of our church, but something was missing. It was not until his baptism on All Saints' Day six months later that we experienced the powerful sense of fulfillment from publicly offering our thanks to God in the midst of the church community.

When our second son was born, we were better prepared. We had made arrangements with our priest and the chaplain at the hospital to gather with us in the hospital room the day after his birth so that we could offer thanks to God for his arrival in our lives. The priest adapted a simple service based on the rite for A Thanksgiving for the Birth or Adoption of a Child, and we gathered around my hospital bed with John sleeping peacefully through it all. The opportunity to give thanks so soon after the miraculous experience of birth was for us a sacramental moment that became an integral part of welcoming John into the world, a way of expressing our awareness of God's presence at this time in our lives.

The service of thanksgiving in our prayer book today is based on Jewish and early Christian rites of purification after childbirth and of welcome extended to the newborn. Some medieval rites were familiarly known as the "churching of women," and included prayers, psalms, communion, and sprinkling the woman with holy water. The 1552 Book of Common Prayer changed the title and focus of the service to The Thanksgiving of Women after Childbirth. Further revisions were made in subsequent prayer books. The 1928 prayer book, for example, added a prayer for the child as well as the mother and thus continued the trend toward making this service one of thanksgiving for the child rather than the reincorporation of the mother into the community.

The rite in the 1979 prayer book has eliminated all references to any ritual impurity brought on by childbirth, and focuses instead on giving thanks for the gift of a child to a family, either by birth or adoption. This rite is thus a good example of the way pastoral liturgies adapt to changing times, circumstances, and societies over time, ensuring that they actually address the real needs and concerns of people in different cultures and ages.

This liturgy is intended to take place in the context of a Sunday Eucharist or service of Morning Prayer, "as soon as convenient after the birth of a child, or after receiving a child by adoption," in order for the family to "be welcomed by the congregation and to give thanks to Almighty God" (BCP 439). Usually it is incorporated into the Eucharist just before the offertory, when the child and his or her family are invited to come forward and stand before the altar.

One of the most beautiful prayers for families is contained within this service, adapted from the prayer for the child added in the 1928 prayer book. It is well worth praying often throughout the sometimes long and difficult years of child rearing:

We give you thanks for the blessing you have bestowed upon this family in giving them a child. Confirm their joy by a lively sense of your presence with them, and give them calm strength and patient wisdom as they seek to bring this child to love all that is true and noble, just and pure, lovable and gracious, excellent and admirable, following the example of our Lord and Savior, Jesus Christ. *Amen.* (BCP 443)

Other prayers that are useful for parents to know are included at the end of the rite, such as thanksgiving for a safe delivery, for wise and shared parenting of the child by the couple, and for the child before and after baptism (BCP 444–45).

An abbreviated version of the liturgy may be offered in the hospital or at home, remembering always that those who gather with the new parents and child represent the entire Christian community. Also, as an effort to support women throughout their pregnancy, a simple rite called the Blessing of a Pregnant Woman is included in *The Book of Occasional Services* (BOS 157–58), and may be used privately or at a public service.

THE RECONCILIATION OF A PENITENT

Every society draws limits around human behavior, identifying acts that endanger others or disrupt the life of the community in some way and requiring penalties for those who commit those acts. After the guilty person acknowledges the wrongdoing and pays the appropriate penalty, he or she may be restored to a place within the community. In the church this process takes place through the sacrament of confession and reconciliation.

In Judaism and the early church, certain offenses were disciplined by excommunication—casting the offender out of the community until confession and restitution were made, at which time the individual would be restored through a rite of readmission into the fellowship. These disciplinary measures took place in public rites involving prayer, fasting, the imposition of ashes, and the laying on of hands. Many of our Lenten traditions have their roots in these early practices.

The practice of private confession developed in the Celtic church of the sixth century, as a supplement to the public penance for sins that brought scandal or harm to others in the church. Private penance was intended for those "matters of conscience" known only to the offender and to God. In the Middle Ages the practice of confession and reconciliation was solidified into the form known and so widely caricatured today. It was required prior to communion, not just when the individual was aware of a true need for it, with acts of penance (usually the saying of certain prayers) following the giving of absolution by the priest alone.

At the Reformation, the reformers sought to restore some balance from the earlier practices, allowing lay confessors, for example, and rejecting any hint of "earning" one's forgiveness through the repetition of prayers. They also encouraged public confession through the general confessions in the liturgical celebrations of the church. When such general confessions were not enough, the 1549 prayer book allowed for private confession with an exhortation before receiving communion that is included in modified form in our 1979 book:

> If, in your preparation, you need help and counsel, then go and open your grief to a discreet and understanding priest, and confess your sins, that you may receive the benefit of absolution, and spiritual counsel and advice; to the removal of scruple and doubt, the assurance of pardon, and the strengthening of your faith. (BCP 317)

In the churches of the Anglican Communion, confession is encouraged but not required: "All can; some should; none must" has long been our stance.[69] Since none of the earlier revisions of the Book of Common Prayer had a rite for private confession, however, priests tended to develop their own, often adapting from other traditions such as the Roman Catholic and Eastern Orthodox. The 1979 prayer book includes two forms for reconciliation, one quite simple and the other more elaborate; both are revisions and adaptations of Roman and Byzantine rites.

Both forms for the Reconciliation of a Penitent presuppose that the person seeking reconciliation has spent time reflecting on his or her life. The practice of self-examination is an essential part of any mature spiritual life, for without such ongoing reflection we cannot grow. We practice self-examination throughout our lives whenever we step back and consider where we are, what we are doing, how we are living, what is working well and what is not—in our workplace, our relationships among family and friends, at school or church. Periodically it is important to do the same evaluation of our relationship with God, and over the centuries a number of approaches to doing a "spiritual inventory" have been developed.

Once people have completed some form of self-examination and can articulate those behaviors, patterns, attitudes, or yearnings they wish to confess to God in order to seek absolution and restoration to health, it is time to meet with a priest or lay confessor. Some people find their parish priest to be helpful; others prefer to have a special relationship with someone from beyond their local community, perhaps someone trained in spiritual direction as well. As the prayer book notes, "confession may be heard anytime and anywhere." Although the idea of "going to confession" may evoke images of small confessional boxes with a grated window, in the Episcopal Church you will probably not find these boxes in use. Rather, the priest and penitent usually meet in a quiet place, perhaps sitting in a room together or kneeling at the altar rail or in a side chapel.

The practice of self-examination can be rather intimidating at first, as you review your life and bring to mind ways you may have offended God by your words and actions. How do we know exactly what "sin" is, and what we need to confess? Sometimes our hurtful and damaging actions are quite clear; at other times, we sin not by the things we do, but by the things we have "left undone" (BCP 447). It can all seem quite overwhelming. I well remember making my first confession when I was in college, and it was a daunting task to sift through the previous twenty years—so daunting, in fact, that I ended up with only two or three meager items on a list after a frustrating hour of solitary preparation. And yet despite the inadequacy of the actual confession, it was simply the practice of self-examination and the intention to confess all that had gone before and "start fresh" that mattered. I was grateful for the phrase in the form for confession that included "all other sins which I cannot now remember"! I left the encounter knowing I was forgiven.

Within the rite itself there is an opportunity for counsel, direction, and comfort with the person hearing the confession, and this help can be invaluable precisely because it *is* difficult to discern what actions and inactions are standing in the way of our relationship with God. A wise priest can help us see the patterns our actions make, leading us to the fundamental sin that is at the root rather than focusing too much attention on the forms that sin takes in our lives. For example, though we may see specific instances in which we have procrastinated as something to bring to confession, a confessor might encourage us to look at the pattern of procrastination and the deeper roots of the pattern. Are we struggling with a fear of failure, born of an inability to trust in God's love for us? Are we suffering from depression, or overwhelming burnout? Are we unconsciously aware that we in fact do not think the task is the right thing to do, and yet are afraid to trust our instinct and speak that truth? It is to these deeper issues that a confessor will usually turn our attention.

Both of the two forms of the rite of reconciliation in the 1979 prayer book follow the same pattern: acknowledgment that we have sinned; an invitation to confession; the confession of sin, with space for the identification of specific sins; a time of counsel, direction, and comfort; the giving and receiving of absolution; and a dismissal. The rite can be quite short and to the point, or it may involve some conversation as the priest and penitent seek to restore the relationship with God and bring some closure to the areas of sin being addressed. The actual confession may consist of one specific thing for which forgiveness is needed, or it may consist of a list of several behaviors or attitudes that are the signs of sin's presence in a person's life.

Some people incorporate confession into their spiritual discipline on several occasions throughout the liturgical year, perhaps during Lent and Advent, and before certain feast days. Others come only when they have a particular need to hear the assurance of forgiveness and to benefit from the wisdom, experience, and discernment of another Christian, such as in times of crisis or transition. Some people never come, finding the opportunity for confession provided in the public confessions of the church's liturgies adequate. In the Anglican tradition, with its emphasis on formation in holiness and the sanctification of every aspect of our lives, each of us must determine our own readiness to enter into the rite of reconciliation. When we do, we will find our faith strengthened by the confessor's concluding words to us, assuring us of the unbounded and freely given forgiveness of a God who seeks only our wholeness and fullness of life:

> Now there is rejoicing in heaven; for you were lost, and are found; you were dead, and are now alive in Christ Jesus our Lord. Abide in peace. The Lord has put away all your sins. *Thanks be to God.* (BCP 451)

MINISTRATION TO THE SICK

Illness and death are an unavoidable facet of human existence: while we live as embodied creatures on this earth, there will be times when our bodies suffer disease and injury, and eventually each one of us will face the moment at which our bodies cease to live and breathe. All religious traditions take the reality of bodily suffering and death into account, and seek to offer those who are sick or dying solace and comfort, strength, and some means of coping. Some traditions believe in the power of prayer to heal the body; others focus on the power of prayer to help the sick person endure his or her suffering with grace.

As Christians we follow a Lord who came among us healing those he touched, restoring the skin of lepers, bringing sight to a man born blind, curing illnesses of the mind, even raising the dead. Healing—

physical, mental, or spiritual—is at the very heart of the gospel: Jesus came that we might be made whole. And so Christians have continued Jesus' ministry of praying for one another in times of sickness, asking that God's healing grace would be present in every situation where there is illness, suffering, or death. At times healing takes place beyond the knowledge of human medicine, and the source of healing could only be the mysterious grace of God that sustains our lives. More often, for many of us the healings we experience or witness are not as dramatic as those recorded in the gospels and the Acts of the Apostles; rather, God's healing grace comes through the seemingly ordinary miracles of medicine. Yet it is God's grace nonetheless, as the power of prayer surrounds those who are sick with the strength they need to be healed.

Since bodily suffering and death are such universal human experiences, the prayer book includes a variety of options within the rite for the Ministration to the Sick, as well as a separate rite for Ministration at the Time of Death. The rite for Ministration to the Sick is divided into three parts: Ministry of the Word, the Laying on of Hands and Anointing, and Holy Communion. Depending on the needs of the person for whom prayer is offered, the service may be brief, with only a few prayers and a short reading. At other times a more elaborate service may be helpful, including a number of Scripture readings, an opportunity for the confession of sin, the laying on of hands or anointing with oil, and Holy Communion. These rites may be performed with only the sick person and the priest or lay minister present, or other members of the family, friends, or medical staff may join in.

A number of prayers for specific intentions are also provided, such as prayers for recovery from sickness, for a sick child, for nurses and doctors, for the "sanctification of illness," and before an operation (BCP 458–60). New to the 1979 prayer book are a selection of prayers that may be used privately by the sick person, prayers for trust in God, for relief of pain, for the gift of sleep for "the refreshing of soul and body," and for courage to face the day to come (BCP 461). There are also a number of prayers and blessings, a litany of healing, and helpful Scripture readings for those who are sick or suffering in A Public Service of Healing found in *The Book of Occasional Services* (BOS 166–73).

The opening rubric for the service of Ministration to the Sick raises an important point about this rite and indeed about all the liturgical ministries of the church: "In case of illness, the Minister of the Congregation is to be notified," it states simply (BCP 453). The sacraments of the church are freely available to all who seek them, and yet they are often left unaccepted simply because we do not ask for them. In the confusion of illness the priest is sometimes not told of the sick person's need for prayer, or we hesitate to ask for the priest's time because we wrongly assume that our needs are less important than those of others. Clergy almost invariably welcome the opportunity to pray for those who are sick or suffering, but they are not mind readers. When we consider our desire for the prayerful support of the church community, we need to remember Jesus' words to his disciples: "Ask, and it will be given you; search, and you will find; knock, and the door will be opened for you" (Matt 7:7). We will receive God's healing grace through the prayer and anointing of the church only if we ask.

MINISTRATION AT THE TIME OF DEATH

In his *Commentary on the American Prayer Book*, Marion Hatchett notes that by the fourth century "the practice of giving communion to the dying as a means of *viaticum* (sustenance for the journey) seems to have been regarded as an ancient custom."[70] Praying with and for those who are dying has thus been Christian practice for centuries; in fact, at times in the church's liturgical tradition the emphasis on praying for the dying and offering them "last rites," including "extreme unction" or anointing with oil just before death, has overshadowed prayers for healing. Twentieth-century revisions to the prayer book—and advances in medical science that make it reasonable for us to expect the sick person to recover—restored this ancient focus on healing for the sick. Although many of the prayers and the rite for Holy Communion in the Ministration to the Sick may well be appropriate for the dying as well, the 1979 prayer book includes a separate section of prayers specifically to be used at the time of death.

The forms of prayer in Ministration at the Time of Death include a litany that may be prayed by members of the family and friends, as well as a shortened version of an early English (or Sarum) commendation:

> Depart, O Christian soul, out of this world;
> In the Name of God the Father Almighty who created you;
> In the Name of Jesus Christ who redeemed you;
> In the Name of the Holy Spirit who sanctifies you.
> May your rest be this day in peace,
> and your dwelling place in the Paradise of God. (BCP 464)

Prayers for a Vigil are also included, to be used when needed between the moment of death and the funeral, such as when family members and friends are gathered at the funeral home or the family home. In the Middle Ages a vigil was a normal part of the burial liturgy, and in some cultures this tradition (commonly known by its English name, "wake") remains essential to the rites surrounding a death in the family.

Finally, the 1979 prayer book includes a new form of prayer for the Reception of the Body into the church, which is especially useful when the body arrives at the church prior to the service to allow for a vigil or visitation. It includes prayers for the person who has died, as well as a prayer for those who are bereaved.

The Burial of the Dead

The death of a Christian is an occasion for both sorrow and rejoicing. While we grieve the loss of beloved members of our family or community and miss their presence among us, we celebrate that they are now in the "blessed rest of everlasting peace," a part of the "glorious company of the saints in light" (BCP 499). The prayer book notes that "baptized Christians are properly buried from the church," rather than a funeral home, at a time when other members of the congregation can be present (BCP 468).

The rubrics for the burial office further remind us that the order for burial is "an Easter liturgy" that "finds all its meaning in the resurrection": "Because Jesus was raised from the dead, we, too, shall be raised" (BCP 507). We may experience profound feelings of loss, anger, sadness, fear, and loneliness, but as Christians we abide in the knowledge that not even death can separate us from the love of God in Christ Jesus. The burial office is thus not in fact what many people mean when they call the funeral a "memorial service": it is indeed a time to memorialize or remember the person who has died, but its primary focus is to celebrate the resurrection into eternal life in which the person has now participated.

Because every individual is unique, with particular gifts and difficult traits and a lifetime of associations and relationships within the human community, every funeral is different. The funeral for an elderly great-grandmother who has lived a full life and whose mind and body were failing can be the occasion of great thanksgiving for the person she was and all she accomplished in her long life. The death of an infant or small child, on the other hand, can be a heartwrenching and seemingly unbearable loss for those who were able to cherish that small life for such a short time. And in between the very old and very young there is an infinite variety of people whose deaths mean something distinctive for those who knew and loved them.

For this reason, three different forms for burial are provided in the 1979 Book of Common Prayer, to allow for as much specificity as possible while still maintaining the primary focus of the office on the Christian hope of the resurrection. Rite One of the burial office is in the traditional, Elizabethan language adapted from the early prayer books many elderly Episcopalians grew up knowing and loving, while Rite Two is in contemporary language and offers additional options for anthems, prayers, and readings. The third Order for Burial, new to this prayer book, is simply an outline of the service, giving wide discretion to the priest when "for pastoral considerations, neither of the burial rites in this Book is deemed appropriate" (BCP 506). In both Rite One and Rite Two, prayers particularly intended for use at the burial of a child are also provided, and certain Scripture lessons are recommended for such a difficult occasion. *Enriching Our Worship 2* likewise offers prayers for use at the burial of a child.

In general, the burial office follows the order of service for the Eucharist, with specific adaptations, of course. The rite opens with the singing or saying of anthems, usually as the closed coffin, covered with a white pall, is brought to the front of the church. If the body has been cremated, an urn or suitable container for the ashes may be placed near the altar. After the opening, prayer readings from Scripture are heard and several psalms are sung or said. A homily is preached and the Apostles' Creed (which reminds us of our baptismal faith) is said. Several forms for the prayers of the people are provided, focusing on the communion of saints and the Christian hope of resurrection, as well as the grief experienced by those who mourn.

After communion, if a Eucharist is celebrated as part of the burial office, the prayers of the Commendation are said just before the body (or container of ashes) is removed from the church for burial. The Commendation was added to the 1979 prayer book because it has become an increasingly common situation that not everyone at the funeral will be able to accompany the body to the graveside or columbarium for the committal. The Commendation thus provides a sense of closure for those who must leave at this point. Anthems with their powerful reminder of the Christian hope again accompany the body as it is carried out of the church:

Christ is risen from the dead, trampling down death by death, and giving life to those in the tomb. . . .

The Lord will guide our feet into the way of peace, having taken away the sin of the world. . . .

Into paradise may the angels lead you.
At your coming may the martyrs receive you,
and bring you into the holy city Jerusalem. (BCP 500)

The final part of the burial office is the Committal, which takes place at the graveside or at the columbarium, or wherever the ashes are to be interred or scattered. It is a brief service, with an anthem and prayers allowing for a final farewell to the loved one's body, "earth to earth, ashes to ashes, dust to dust." And yet we leave the burial office with the sure and certain hope that "he who raised Jesus Christ from the dead will also give new life to our mortal bodies through his indwelling Spirit." So although "in the midst of life we are in death," we are still able to affirm, "My heart, therefore, is glad, and my spirit rejoices; my body also shall rest in hope" (BCP 492, 501).

QUESTIONS FOR REFLECTION AND DISCUSSION

1. If you have children, in what ways have the prayers and liturgies of the church touched your experience of giving birth to, adopting, or raising them? What was most helpful? What was missing?

2. What is your view and experience of private confession? If you decide you would like to participate in the rite of reconciliation, what steps would you need to take?

3. What has been your experience of the church at times of illness and death? How have those experiences affected your faith as a Christian? When you have been ill, have you ever asked for prayer? If so, in what ways were those prayers helpful, or not? Have you attended funerals in an Episcopal church? What did you learn from participating in the burial office?

Tools for Prayer and Study
The Lectionary, Prayers, Catechism, and Historical Documents

*Blessed Lord, who caused all holy Scriptures to be written for our
learning: Grant us so to hear them, read, mark, learn, and
inwardly digest them, that we may embrace and ever hold fast the
blessed hope of everlasting life, which you have given us in our
Savior Jesus Christ; who lives and reigns with you and the Holy
Spirit, one God, for ever and ever.* Amen.

(BCP 236)

In addition to its collection of prayers and liturgical rites for use
throughout the church year, the 1979 Book of Common Prayer
includes several tools to help us in our study of Scripture and our
understanding of the Christian faith within the Anglican tradition. In
this chapter we will consider some of the tools Episcopalians tend to
use most frequently as we seek to live our faith and grow in Christ.

THE LECTIONARY

Since many of the first Christians were Jews, the selection of
Scripture passages used in the church's earliest gatherings for wor-
ship, prayer, and the hearing of God's word were those used in the
Jewish synagogues. Soon, however, they began adding readings from
Christian writings (such as the gospels and the letters of Paul and
other apostles, some of which later became our New Testament) to

127

those of the Hebrew Scriptures (we call some of these writings the
Old Testament). Gradually, Christian lectionaries—books containing the passages from the Bible selected for public worship—were
developed to provide a pattern to these readings. As the church year
of seasons, feasts, and fasts took shape in the following centuries,
readings with particular themes were assigned to certain holy days.
Over the course of "non-holy" or ordinary days, entire books of the
Bible were read straight through from beginning to end. The oldest
liturgical lectionary we have dates back to the seventh century, and
includes readings from the Christian epistles and gospels.

Over the centuries the church has continued to discuss the best
ways to incorporate the reading of Scripture into the worship and
study of Christians. As an alternative to following the suggested
readings in a lectionary, for example, the early English reformer John
Wycliffe believed that we should simply read the Bible straight
through, from Genesis to Revelation, since in his view every book
was equal in importance. Some Reformation churches elected to
leave the choice of Scripture passages for a service entirely up to the
worship leader or local community, who could choose readings
based on the needs or interests of that day.

Many Christian denominations and independent congregations
today likewise do not use a lectionary system of Scripture reading,
but rather leave the choice up to the discretion of the pastor or
minister, or perhaps a worship committee. There is of course some
benefit to this flexibility, which allows for spontaneity and a close
tailoring of the readings to current events and community needs. On
the other hand, it can also be tempting to focus only on the positive,
"easy" readings and neglect the harder, more puzzling passages. The
biblical scholar Marianne Micks has noted that in our day "a large pro-
portion of Christendom . . . has chosen a solution midway between
these extremes of form and freedom—the solution of a lectionary, a
fixed selection of biblical readings geared to the church year." She goes
on to describe some of the benefits of using a lectionary:

> The use of a lectionary has at least two major advantages over
> reading straight through a given book, including all the genealogi-
> cal tables and cultic laws of ancient Israel, or listening only to the

pastor's favorite passages. It more readily relates the readings to one another, so that the Old Testament lesson illuminates the New, and the New enriches the Old. It also powerfully invites us to enter into the annual cycle commemorating the mighty acts of God in Christ.[71]

Many lectionaries have been created, revised, and revised again over the centuries, some with several lengthy readings designated for each service, others with only one or two brief extracts. The lectionaries used at the time of the earliest prayer books were based on the English Sarum liturgical tradition, and if an Anglican attended every Sunday service he or she would hear almost the entire Old Testament read in seven years, and all the books of the New Testament except for the Revelation to John in a little over two years. The Psalter would be heard twice every year.

In subsequent revisions of the prayer book, changes were also made to the lectionary. The ecumenical movements of the second half of the twentieth century led to a shared reading of Scripture in worship as well, with the current lectionaries for all the liturgical denominations today having certain elements in common. Our Episcopal lectionary is a new revision of the lectionary adopted by the Roman Catholic Church after Vatican II. The Old Testament, psalm, epistle, and gospel readings you will hear during the Sunday Eucharist at an Episcopal church today are normally taken from this lectionary, found at the back of prayer book (BCP 887–931). A separate Daily Office Lectionary is also provided for use at Morning and Evening Prayer (BCP 933–1001). If you attend services every Sunday, you will hear much of the Old Testament and nearly all of the New Testament in three years.

The lectionary for the readings for Sunday mornings is divided into a three-year cycle, called Years A, B, and C, centered on the reading of the gospels. These passages are read during the first half of the Eucharist (the Liturgy of the Word), or at Morning Prayer if it is the main Sunday service in a congregation. Portions of the Gospel of John are read during every Lent and Easter season, while one of the three other gospels is read during the rest of the church year—Matthew in Year A, Mark in Year B, and Luke in Year C. The content of the reading from the Old Testament and the psalm is often linked to the gospel, while the passages from the epistles are usually read in course from start to finish or are selected because of their association with a particular season in the church year.

For the Fourth Sunday of Advent, to choose a particularly clear example, we hear the story of Joseph learning that Mary, his betrothed, was expecting a child. When Joseph decided to "dismiss her quietly" so as not to provoke a scandal, an angel intervened to reassure him. "All this took place to fulfill what had been spoken by the Lord through the prophet," Matthew concludes. And he then quotes from the prophet Isaiah the well-known promise stating that a "virgin shall conceive and bear a son" (Matt 1:18–25). The reading from the Old Testament is the very passage from Isaiah that Matthew quotes (Isa 7:10–17)—clearly intended to connect to the gospel reading. The epistle reading is from Paul's Letter to the Romans, and its direct link to the gospel, like most of the epistle readings in the lectionary, is less obvious.

In addition to the Sunday readings, the prayer book lectionary also provides readings for saints' and holy days, and for various occasions. The saints commemorated in the Episcopal Church have their own lections, and when they are saints from biblical times, their readings usually include the passages referring to them. The gospel reading for the feast day of Saint Thomas on December 21, for example, describes the incident that earned him the dubious distinction of being called "doubting Thomas": "Unless I see the mark of the nails in his hands, and put my finger in the mark of the nails and my hand in his side," Thomas declares to the other disciples after they report they have seen Jesus alive again, "I will not believe" (John 20:25).

When you attend a special service such as a church convention, confirmation, or ordination, the readings from the Bible that you hear will be taken from the list of propers (assigned lessons and prayers) for Various Occasions (BCP 927–31). Some of the lessons given are less clearly linked to certain liturgies or occasions but rather are thematic, to be read when the intention of a certain service has a specific focus. There are propers given For the Mission of the Church, for example, For Education, For Social Justice, and For Vocation in Daily Work.

The Daily Office Lectionary, which follows the lectionary for Sundays, holy days, and various occasions in the prayer book, provides guidance for reading these more substantial passages from Scripture. The selections of readings in this lectionary tend to be more "in course," reading a book from start to finish. While the Sunday lectionary is a three-year cycle, the Daily Office Lectionary is a two-year cycle, called Year One and Year Two. As with the seasons of the church year, the Daily Office Lectionary begins with the week of the First Sunday of Advent. These readings can be used with any of the hours of prayer offered throughout the day: usually two of the lessons are chosen for Morning Prayer, and the remaining lesson saved for Evening Prayer. Alternatively, if additional readings are needed on a particular day, then they may be borrowed from the other year's cycle. If only one Daily Office is prayed that day, then all three readings could be used. As with the Sunday lectionary, we are free to shorten or lengthen any of the readings in the Daily Office Lectionary when a certain verse calls for more reflection, or when we wish to follow a particular story or theological argument in the assigned reading further. The point is to "read, mark, learn, and inwardly digest" the Word of God, not to complete an assignment.

In the Episcopal Church we have become so accustomed to hearing Scripture passages selected from the Old Testament, Psalms, New Testament, and Gospels read at our worship services that we can sometimes forget that having a lectionary does not in any way preclude the discipline of reading a book of the Bible straight through as John Wycliffe suggested, some of the shorter books perhaps in one sitting. Fresh insights and deeper understanding can be gained by reading even familiar passages in their context, and reading the Bible quietly in private offers more space for undivided attention and reflection than is sometimes afforded in a crowded service.

There are any number of Bible study methods, from Ignatian to African to *lectio divina*. Many of us use the lectionary as a basis for our study of Scripture, but that does not mean we cannot incorporate a variety of methods into our prayer and study in order to deepen our understanding. Well into her nineties, my grandmother embarked on what would be her final reading of the entire Bible from Genesis to Revelation, after a lifetime of studying and teaching the Bible to others. The lectionary does not constrain our learning only to certain passages or prevent our rumination on a single verse, but simply provides a helpful framework for the practice of being formed and informed by God's Word.

Prayers and Thanksgivings

This section of the 1979 Book of Common Prayer is a compilation of a number of various prayers and thanksgivings that were scattered throughout earlier prayer books, as well as a substantial number of new prayers—thirty-eight new prayers, two new graces, and nine new thanksgivings, to be exact.[72]

The first prayer book of 1549 included only two extra prayers, one for rain (which is included in our prayer book on page 828) and one for fair weather. In subsequent revisions other prayers were added according to the pressing concerns of the age: prayers for use in time of famine, plague, or war; a prayer of thanksgiving for the ending of "seditious tumults"; prayers for various forms of government; prayers for prisoners; prayers for the return of those at sea; and prayers for church missionaries. In the 1979 prayer book the various prayers and thanksgivings are grouped according to theme and numbered in an index for ease of use (BCP 810–13).

These prayers are useful for both individuals and congregations. The prayers for birthdays and graces before meals, for example, can be incorporated into family celebrations; the prayers for guidance, quiet confidence, and protection are helpful in private times of prayer or in the context of spiritual direction. The prayer for church musicians and artists can be offered in the midst of a Sunday Eucharist in thanksgiving for the ministry of the choir, and the prayers for the church can be said at the meetings of small prayer or Bible study groups. The prayers for the president and Congress and for sound government can be said near the times of elections or in the midst of national crises.

We are acutely aware of our human needs, which makes it easy to focus on prayers of intercession. So the offering of thanksgiving is sometimes the most neglected dimension of our prayer. The prayers of thanksgiving offered in this section can be salutary reminders of

God's care for us and the many gifts we have already been given. They can also be springboards for our own thanksgivings for the grace of God apparent in our individual lives and in the world around us. The prayer of thanksgiving for the gift of a child is one of my favorites, and can be prayed by parents throughout the years of child rearing:

> Heavenly Father, you sent your own Son into this world. We thank you for the life of this child, entrusted to our care. Help us to remember that we are all your children, and so to love and nurture him, that he may attain to that full stature intended for him in your eternal kingdom; for the sake of your dear Son, Jesus Christ our Lord. *Amen.* (BCP 841)

An Outline of the Faith

After the collection of additional prayers and thanksgivings, the 1979 Book of Common Prayer provides a section titled "An Outline of the Faith, commonly called the Catechism." A form of teaching has been included in previous prayer books, and the Outline of the Faith provided in the 1979 book is a substantially expanded and revised version of these catechisms.

The word "catechism" probably dates to the Reformation age, when the desire for church reform and theological clarity and revision prompted both Protestants and Catholics to formulate teaching guides and manuals of instruction in the faith. Most, including Luther's Short Catechism of 1529, were based on the creeds, the Lord's Prayer, and the Ten Commandments; some also included an exposition of the sacraments.

In the 1549 Book of Common Prayer, catechetical instructions are included within the rites for baptism and confirmation, with questions and answers for the bishop to ask confirmands concerning the effects of baptism, the doctrine of the Trinity, the Ten Commandments, and the Lord's Prayer. In the 1604 Book of Common Prayer, a section on the sacraments was added, and in the 1662 prayer book the catechism was moved from the confirmation rite and placed in its own section. Questions on the ministry, the church, and what it means to be a church member were added in the American prayer book of 1928, and the entire catechism was then expanded, rearranged, and revised in the 1979 book.

The notes concerning the catechism in the 1979 prayer book state that this catechism has two intended uses. First, it is a teaching aid for clergy and lay catechists, "to give an outline for instruction," perhaps for confirmation classes or newcomers to the Episcopal Church. It cautions that the catechism is not a "complete statement of belief and practice" but rather "a point of departure for the teacher," who can use its question-and-answer format as a way of beginning a discussion on various aspects of the Christian faith and life.

It is common knowledge that we learn best when we ask questions as well as receive information, and most teachers find it helpful to allow space for exploration and discussion between the questions and answers formulated by the catechism. Many of us remember catechism or confirmation classes from our youth in which we were expected to memorize the answers in the catechism in order to pass our "test" at confirmation. Times have changed, however, and the 1979 prayer book suggests the catechism is provided "for ease of reference" (BCP 844), not for memorization and recitation.

The second use suggested by the prayer book concerns those who are new to the Episcopal Church, "to provide a brief summary of the Church's teaching for an inquiring stranger who picks up a Prayer Book" (BCP 844). Since the first encounter many people have with the Episcopal Church is an occasion when they attend one of our liturgical services—baptism, marriage, burial, perhaps a Sunday Eucharist—it makes sense to include a general outline of what we believe within the covers of the first book newcomers will hold during their visit.

The catechism is well worth reading in its entirety and studying more closely section by section, either on our own or in a class. It poses fundamental questions we have all asked at one time or another: "What does it mean to be created in the image of God?"; "What is sin?"; "What is prayer?" It also asks questions we may not have thought of yet, but that help us make sense of what we practice and give words to what we already believe: "Why do we praise God?"; "What are the principal kinds of prayer?"; "What is required of us at Baptism?" For those of us who find the vocabulary of the catechism daunting, however, as well as those of us intensely interested in the necessary and important quest for theological understanding, the liturgical scholar Leonel Mitchell offers a salutary reminder that complete understanding of theological principles is not required for participation in the liturgies and sacraments of the church. In the liturgy, he notes, we are given "the words and means" to be united with God. "And union with God," he concludes, "not deeper understanding, is the only thing essential for new life in Christ."[73]

HISTORICAL DOCUMENTS

Tucked in between the catechism and the lectionary in the 1979 prayer book is a section called the Historical Documents of the Church. Three of these five documents—the Athanasian Creed, the Preface to the first Book of Common Prayer, and the Thirty-Nine Articles—have been included in a number of previous prayer books, while the Chalcedonian Definition and the Chicago-Lambeth Quadrilateral are new to this revision. They are included in the prayer book because they "have milestone importance in the history of Christian thought,"[74] but are particularly significant for Anglicans and Episcopalians as we have come to understand our faith over the centuries.

It is a mark of the passing of time through history that when many of these documents were developed, the people involved in their discernment and crafting argued, fought, and even died for the theologies the documents describe. Today they cease to be the focus of controversy, and are in fact largely unknown to many Anglicans throughout the world today, relegated to a small section at the back of the prayer book. Indeed, as Archbishop Michael Ramsey once noted during a lecture at a seminary in Wisconsin, the print for the Thirty-Nine Articles is "so small I have to put on my glasses in order to read them!"[75] And yet they are foundational to our faith, and even a casual reading of these documents can give a glimpse of the theological riches of Anglicanism. A close study with others who can help to interpret some of the difficult language of their historical and theological context bears even more fruit. We then discover that although the issues and ways of speaking about them may have changed, controversies and vigorous discussions about what we believe and how we are to follow Christ in community have been part of the church's life from the beginning.

The Chalcedonian Definition

During the first five centuries of the church's life, Christians struggled to define what they believed to be true about God, Jesus, and the Holy Spirit. The church was by no means united in its understanding of these things, any more than it is today. So church leaders met regularly in councils to discuss the various theologies being set forth by bishops or other theologians, and to seek to define the limits of orthodoxy, or "right believing." The Chalcedonian Definition—officially called The Definition of the Union of the Divine and Human Natures in the Person of Christ—was developed at the Council of Chalcedon in 451 C.E., the same council that affirmed the Nicene Creed created by an earlier council, the creed we use in our services of the Eucharist today.

The council members meeting at Chalcedon were particularly concerned with the theologies posed by two leaders, Nestorius and Eutyches. Nestorius was a bishop of Constantinople who preached a sermon stating that in Christ there were two separate persons, one human and the other divine. He therefore did not think it possible for God to be "born" of a human mother, as the popular term used for Mary, *Theotokos* or "Godbearer," implied. The human part of Jesus was born of Mary, he argued, but the divine part was eternal. His suggestion that a more precise term for Mary would be *Christokos* was received with outrage, however, since by the fifth century Mary was the center of focus for many Christians as the one who knew intimately "the paradoxical glory of God as an infant."[76]

In complete opposition to Nestorius's position, the monk Eutyches offered the rather extreme position that in fact Christ had only one nature, and that his human nature was completely transformed by its union with the divine in the incarnation. This belief made sense to those who understood the purpose of the Incarnation to be the divinization of humanity: in our union with Christ through our prayers and devotional practice of the spiritual life we could become like God.

The Chalcedonian Definition sought to define the middle ground of what we believe to be true about the Incarnation between these two poles on either side. It was gathered from letters among various bishops discussing these issues, and is thus not a final statement of a theological position; rather, it seeks to define the "limits of speculation."[77] A theologian from our own day, Rebecca Lyman, eloquently describes the powerful theological mystery the leaders at Chalcedon were trying to uphold:

> When we contemplate Christ, we see the fullness of divine nature and the fullness of human nature: we see the face of God and we see our own face as it should become. In this one person we can contemplate the mystery of God revealed and the mystery of ourselves redeemed.[78]

The Athanasian Creed

Most scholars believe the creed commonly known as the Athanasian Creed was written in southern Gaul late in the fifth century, but its theology concerning God as Trinity is believed to express the faith of the great fourth-century bishop and theologian Athanasius. In the Middle Ages it became a regular part of the liturgical prayers of Christians in the Western church, and was likewise included in the early Anglican prayer books for use on certain feast days.

The newly formed Episcopal Church declined to include the Athanasian Creed in the first American Book of Common Prayer, however, and the 1979 prayer book is the first to include it, though it does so as a historical document and not as a creed to be recited in worship. The words of a letter written by Bishop Samuel Seabury soon after the publication of the 1789 prayer book reveal some of the confusion surrounding this creed, as well as his hope for inclusion that has been fulfilled in our own day:

> With regard to the propriety of reading the Athanasian Creed in Church, I was never fully convinced. With regard to the

impropriety of banishing it out of the Prayer-book I am clear. . . . And I do hope, though possibly I hope in vain, that Christian charity and love of union will one day bring that Creed into this book, were it only to stand as articles of faith stand; and to show that we do not renounce the Catholic doctrine of the Trinity as held in the Western Church.[79]

As Scabury notes, the "Catholic doctrine of the Trinity" is at the heart of this creed: "The Catholic Faith is this: That we worship one God in Trinity, and Trinity in Unity, neither confounding the Persons, nor dividing the Substance" (BCP 864). Even in this simple summary we see, however, that the language of this creed can be complex and often needs interpretation for those of us who live in another age.

Preface to the First Book of Common Prayer (1549)

This preface written by Archbishop Thomas Cranmer as a rationale for the revision of the liturgical rites for the Daily Office has been included in subsequent prayer books, perhaps because it is an eloquent expression of the theology undergirding the Anglican practice of common prayer. Some of the foundational principles of prayer book revision that guide us today are contained (and admittedly sometimes well hidden!) in these paragraphs.

Cranmer notes first that the offices of prayer were "not ordained, but of a good purpose, and for a great advancement of godliness" (BCP 866)—thus establishing the ground for revision of these prayers of the church rather than seeing them as divinely ordained and unchangeable. He then goes on to recognize that "this godly and decent order of the ancient fathers" had been so "altered, broken, and neglected" that the daily offices from the early church stood in need of restoration and revision. This return to the simplicity and vigor of the prayers of the early church is a hallmark of the Book of Common Prayer, perhaps nowhere more clearly seen than in our own 1979 revision.

Cranmer further notes that although there must be "some rules" for an ordering of common prayer, these rules should be "few in number" and they should be "plain and easy to be understood" (BCP 866). Instead of a vast array of liturgical books, only the prayer book and the Bible were needed for church services in local parishes, thus easing the burden so that "the people shall not be at so great charge for books, as in time past they have been" (BCP 867). And "all things shall be read and sung in the church in the English tongue, to the end that the congregation may be thereby edified"; when prayers are said privately, they may be said "in any language that they themselves do understand" (BCP 867). Anglicans still believe strongly that the prayers of the church are *common* prayers— available to all, said by all, in a language understood by all.

Finally, in his preface Cranmer addresses the reluctance many of us have to embrace changes in the words and manner of our prayers—a reluctance experienced in the extreme at the time Cranmer was writing. We too find it comforting to pray in ways that are familiar, when we can "say many things by heart" after years of repetition. And yet he believes the great "profit in knowledge" gained by making such revisions to the prayer book are well worth the pain involved, and he trusts that the value of having a single book for common prayer will far outweigh the cost.

Articles of Religion

The Articles of Religion are known familiarly as the Thirty-Nine Articles because there are thirty-nine of them now, although the number varied considerably as they were developed and revised alongside many other Protestant confessions of faith at the time of the Reformation. Like the prayer book, they are largely the work of Archbishop Cranmer, and are moderate in their stance, taking a position in the middle between the Roman Catholics on one extreme and the Anabaptists on the other. The liturgical scholar Massey Shepherd has commented that the Articles are "Protestant to the extent that they do not claim any doctrines as necessary to salvation" except those found in Scripture, and they are Catholic "in the sense that they do not reject the developed traditions of the undivided Church of the early centuries."[80]

Today, as Archbishop Michael Ramsey has noted, the "doctrinal bonds" of the Thirty-Nine Articles have seriously weakened over the centuries since they were written, and today they are largely seen as "venerated historical documents rather than as contemporary confessions."⁸¹ They were in a sense a way of outlining the parameters of Anglican faith and practice in the formative decades after the Reformation, just as the early church councils sought to do in the realm of Christian theology. Anglicanism was formed amidst powerful and often conflicting forces of Puritans and Latitudinarians, Lutherans and Anabaptists, Zwinglians and Roman Catholics. The Thirty-Nine Articles were a way of establishing a common theological ground within which Anglicans could live, much as the prayer book did for worship.

The Articles of Religion we have in our 1979 prayer book are those revised articles adopted after years of consternation and discussion by the American Episcopal Church in 1801 as "the Faith of this Church." Although the Thirty-Nine Articles remain an important foundational statement of belief for Anglicans, they tend for many Episcopalians to be less formative for their faith than the worship and common life of the congregation. Again, as Archbishop Ramsey wisely noted:

> While there are churches in Christendom where, when you ask, "Now, tell us what you stand for?" they will say, "Well, here are our articles, that is what we stand for," it has always been characteristic of Anglicans to reply, "Yes, here are our articles, but here is our Prayer Book as well—come and pray with us, come and worship with us, and that is how you will understand what we stand for."⁸²

The Chicago-Lambeth Quadrilateral 1886, 1888

The liturgical scholar Leonel L. Mitchell aptly describes the Chicago-Lambeth Quadrilateral as "a platform for ecumenical action."⁸³ A growing concern to establish relationships with Christians of other faiths took hold within the Episcopal Church in the second half of the nineteenth century, and combined with similar urgings in other denominations led to much of the significant work toward Christian unity undertaken in the ecumenical movements of the twentieth.

The Quadrilateral was adopted by the bishops of the American Episcopal Church meeting in Chicago in 1886 and by the bishops of the entire Anglican Communion meeting at Lambeth in 1888, and has served as the foundation for the ecumenical efforts of Anglicans ever since. It puts forward one of the key ground rules for ecumenical dialogue:

> This Church does not seek to absorb other Communions, but rather, co-operating with them on the basis of a common Faith and Order, to discountenance schism, to heal the wounds of the Body of Christ, and to promote the charity which is the chief of Christian graces and the visible manifestation of Christ to the world. (BCP 877)

One of the common misconceptions of (and barriers to) ecumenism is that Christian unity requires uniformity and the erasure of our historical, theological, liturgical, and cultural distinctions. Far from it. According to the Chicago-Lambeth Quadrilateral, Christian unity is possible through the cooperative relationships of diverse traditions and practices, united around a common Lord, expressed in a "common Faith and Order."

The four elements of the church that give the statement its name and that are identified as "essential to the restoration of unity among the divided branches of Christendom" (BCP 877) were the work of William Reed Huntington in his book published in 1870 called *The Church Idea*. They are a succinct statement of what we believe is at the core of Christian faith as we have received it. First, we believe in the Bible as the "revealed Word of God." Second, we affirm the Nicene Creed as "the sufficient statement" of the Christian faith. Third, we share in the two biblical sacraments of baptism and Eucharist. And fourth, our ordained ministries include the "Historic Episcopate," though the ministry of the bishop may be "locally adapted" to meet the "varying needs of the nations and peoples called of God into the unity of His Church" (BCP 877). The first three of these elements have been widely shared by many Protestant and Catholic churches alike; the fourth has been the source of more consternation and for many has been a stumbling block to the reunification of the churches. However, in recent years even those barriers have been overcome, and in a time in which the world seems increasingly to be a single "global community," many of us within the Christian churches are coming to realize that what unites us is far more important than what divides us.

QUESTIONS FOR REFLECTION AND DISCUSSION

1. What are some of the methods you have used to study the Bible? Which methods were most effective for you? Why?

2. Turn to the Outline of the Faith in the prayer book, and survey some of the questions. Which ones echo similar questions you have asked, though perhaps in different words? How have your answers differed or resembled the answers given in the catechism?

3. Select one of the Historical Documents to read carefully. What can you learn from this document? What do you find confusing or inconsistent with your own understanding of the faith?

Suggestions for Further Reading

LITURGICAL RESOURCES

The Book of Common Prayer. New York: Church Publishing, 1979.
The current official prayer book of the Episcopal Church.

The Book of Occasional Services. New York: Church Publishing, 2003.
Prayers and liturgical rites authorized by our General Convention for the church year, including lessons and carols for Advent and Christmas, house blessings, and prayers for the catechumenate.

Enriching Our Worship 1: Morning and Evening Prayer, The Great Litany, The Holy Eucharist. New York: Church Publishing, 1998.
Supplemental prayers and liturgical rites in inclusive or expansive language authorized by General Convention.

Enriching Our Worship 2: Ministry with the Sick or Dying, Burial of a Child. New York: Church Publishing, 2000.
Supplemental prayers and liturgical rites in inclusive or expansive language authorized by General Convention.

Lesser Feasts and Fasts. New York: Church Publishing, 2003.
Collects, propers, and brief biographies of the saints commemorated in the Episcopal Church.

143

MUSIC

The Hymnal 1982. New York: Church Publishing, 1985.

Lift Every Voice and Sing II: An African American Hymnal. New York: Church Publishing, 1993.

Voices Found: Women in the Church's Song. New York: Church Publishing, 2003.

We Sing of God: A Hymnal for Children. Edited by Robert N. and Nancy L. Roth. New York: Church Publishing, 1989.

Wonder, Love, and Praise: A Supplement to The Hymnal 1982. New York: Church Publishing, 2001.

THE DAILY OFFICE

Contemporary Office Book. New York: Church Publishing, 1999.
The Daily Office for both years in Rite Two, including complete Scripture readings in the New Revised Standard Version.

Daily Office Book. New York: Church Publishing, 1986.
The Daily Office for both years, including complete Scripture readings in the Revised Standard Version.

Crafton, Barbara Cawthorne. *Let Us Bless the Lord, Year One: Meditations on the Daily Office.* Harrisburg, PA: Morehouse Publishing, 2004.

Tickle, Phyllis. *The Divine Hours: Prayers for Summertime.* New York: Doubleday, 2000.

———. *The Divine Hours: Prayers for Autumn and Wintertime.* New York: Doubleday, 2000.

———. *The Divine Hours: Prayers for Springtime.* New York: Doubleday, 2001.

BOOKS ON LITURGY AND THE PRAYER BOOK

Black, Vicki K. *Welcome to the Church Year: An Introduction to the Seasons of the Episcopal Church.* Harrisburg, PA: Morehouse Publishing, 2004.

Dix, Dom Gregory. *The Shape of the Liturgy.* London and New York: Continuum, 1945.

Galley, Howard E. *The Ceremonies of the Eucharist: A Guide to Celebration.* Cambridge, MA: Cowley Publications, 1989.

Hatchett, Marion J. *Commentary on the American Prayer Book.* Seabury Press: New York, 1981.

———. *The Making of the First American Book of Common Prayer, 1776–1789.* New York: Seabury Press, 1982.

———. *Sanctifying Life, Time and Space: An Introduction to Liturgical Study.* San Francisco: Harper & Row, 1976.

Lee, Jeffrey. *Opening the Prayer Book.* Vol. 7 of *The New Church's Teaching Series.* Cambridge, MA: Cowley Publications, 1999.

Meyers, Ruth A., and Phoebe Pettingell, eds. *Gleanings: Essays on Expansive Language with Prayers for Various Occasions.* New York: Church Publishing, 2001.

Micks, Marianne H. *The Joy of Worship.* New York: Church Publishing, 2004.

Mitchell, Leonel L. *Lent, Holy Week, Easter, and the Great Fifty Days: A Ceremonial Guide.* Cambridge, MA: Cowley Publications, 1996.

———. *Praying Shapes Believing: A Theological Commentary on* The Book of Common Prayer. Harrisburg, PA: Morehouse Publishing, 1985.

————. *Pastoral and Occasional Liturgies: A Ceremonial Guide.* Cambridge, MA: Cowley Publications, 1998.

Plater, Ormonde. *Intercession: A Theological and Practical Guide.* Cambridge, MA: Cowley Publications, 1996.

Price, Charles P., and Louis Weil. *Liturgy for Living.* Rev. ed. Harrisburg, PA: Morehouse Publishing, 1979, 2000.

Russell, Joseph P., ed., *The New Prayer Book Guide to Christian Education.* Rev. ed. Cambridge, MA: Cowley Publications, 1996.

Smith, Martin L., SSJE. *Reconciliation: Preparing for Confession in the Episcopal Church.* Cambridge, MA: Cowley Publications, 1985.

Stuhlman, Byron D. *A Good and Joyful Thing: The Evolution of the Eucharistic Prayer.* New York: Church Publishing, 2000.

————. *Redeeming the Time: An Historical and Theological Study of the Church's Rule of Prayer and the Regular Services of the Church.* New York: Church Publishing, 1992.

Sydnor, William. *The Prayer Book Through the Ages.* Harrisburg, PA: Morehouse Publishing, 1978.

Webber, Christopher L. *Morning Prayer and Baptism,* in the series *A User's Guide to the Book of Common Prayer.* Harrisburg, PA: Morehouse Publishing, 1997.

————. *The Holy Eucharist, Rites I and II,* in the series *A User's Guide to the Book of Common Prayer.* Harrisburg, PA: Morehouse Publishing, 1997.

————. *Welcome to Sunday: An Introduction to Worship in the Episcopal Church.* Harrisburg, PA: Morehouse Publishing, 2003.

————. *Welcome to the Episcopal Church: An Introduction to Its History, Faith, and Worship.* Harrisburg, PA: Morehouse Publishing, 1999.

Weil, Louis. *A Theology of Worship.* Vol. 12 of *The New Church's Teaching Series.* Cambridge, MA: Cowley Publications, 2002.

Notes

1. I owe a debt of gratitude to Rev. Peter Wenner, a priest and colleague in the Diocese of Massachusetts, for his invaluable contributions to this chapter.

2. Charles P. Price and Louis Weil, *Liturgy for Living*, rev. ed. (Harrisburg, PA: Morehouse, 2000), 4.

3. Ibid., 47. The term "collect" may have derived from the position of the prayer at the beginning of the eucharistic service, as a way of "collecting" the people for the Eucharist.

4. Quoted in Ibid., 48.

5. Dom Gregory Dix, *The Shape of the Liturgy* (London and New York: Continuum, 1945), 623.

6. William Sydnor, *The Prayer Book through the Ages* (Harrisburg, PA: Morehouse, 1978), 5.

7. Ibid., 6.

8. Ibid., 11.

9. Ibid., 12–13.

10. Ibid., 13.

11. Marion J. Hatchett, *The Making of the First American Book of Common Prayer, 1776–1789* (New York: Seabury Press, 1982), 112.

12. Quoted in Price and Weil, *Liturgy for Living*, 60.

13. Quoted in Hatchett, *Making of the First American Book of Common Prayer*, 145.

14. Ibid., 148.

15. Jeffrey D. Lee, *Opening the Prayer Book*, vol. 7 of *The New Church's Teaching Series* (Cambridge, MA: Cowley Publications, 1999), 159.

16. Phoebe Pettingell, Introduction to *Enriching Our Worship 1: Morning and Evening Prayer, The Great Litany, The Holy Eucharist* (New York: Church Publishing, 1998), 8.

17. Frank Tracy Griswold, Preface to *Enriching Our Worship 1*, 5.

18. Jennifer M. Phillips, "Praying Rightly: The Poetics of Liturgy," in *Gleanings: Essays on Expansive Language with Prayers for Various Occasions*, ed. Ruth A. Meyers and Phoebe Pettingell (New York: Church Publishing, 2001), 11.

19. Lee, *Opening the Prayer Book*, 149.

20. Ibid., 154–55.

21. Price and Weil, *Liturgy for Living*, 77.

22. From Justin Martyr's *First Apology*, quoted in Aidan Kavanagh, *The Shape of Baptism: The Rite of Christian Initiation* (New York: Pueblo Publishing Company, 1978), 43.

23. Marion J. Hatchett, *Commentary on the American Prayer Book* (New York: Seabury Press, 1981), 253–54.

24. Dix, *Shape of the Liturgy*, 281.

25. Hatchett, *Commentary*, 254.

26. Quoted in Hatchett, *Commentary*, 260.

27. Leonel L. Mitchell, *Praying Shapes Believing: A Theological Commentary on* The Book of Common Prayer (Harrisburg, PA: Morehouse Publishing, 1985), 99.

28. Theophilus of Antioch, quoted in Mitchell, *Praying Shapes Believing*, 107.

29. Dix, *Shape of the Liturgy*, 50–58.

30. Ibid., 58.

31. Justin Martyr, *First Apology*, found in *The Eucharist of the Early Christians* by Willy Rordorf and others (New York: Pueblo Publishing, 1978), 72–73.

32. From Hippolytus, *Apostolic Tradition*, quoted in Price and Weil, *Liturgy for Living*, 133.

33. Ibid., 143.

34. Sydnor, *Prayer Book through the Ages*, 8.

35. Ibid., 10.

36. Michael Ramsey, The *Anglican Spirit*, ed. Dale D. Coleman (New York: Church Publishing, 2004), 6–7.

37. Richard Hooker, *Laws of Ecclesiastical Polity* V. 67. XII.

38. Hatchett, *Commentary*, 324.

39. Ibid., 334.

40. Marianne H. Micks, *Loving the Questions: An Exploration of the Nicene Creed* (New York: Church Publishing, 2005), 3.

41. Micks, *Loving the Questions*, 77.

42. See Ormonde Plater's excellent guide to the Prayers of the People, *Intercession: A Theological and Practical Guide* (Cambridge, MA: Cowley Publications, 1996).

43. Hatchett, *Commentary*, 342.

44. Ibid., 361.

45. *Enriching Our Worship 1*, 60.

46. Quoted in Hatchett, *Commentary*, 384.

47. Hymn 303 in *The Hymnal 1982* (New York: Church Publishing, 1985). Words from the Greek, ca. 110; translated by F. Bland Tucker (1895–1984).

48. *Enriching Our Worship 1*, 70.

49. Dix, *Shape of the Liturgy*, 743–44.

50. William G. Storey, "The Liturgy of the Hours: Cathedral Versus Monastery," in *Christians at Prayer*, ed. John Gallen, S.J. (Notre Dame, IN: University of Notre Dame Press, 1977), 66.

51. Preface to the First Book of Common Prayer (1549), quoted in the 1979 Book of Common Prayer, 866.

52. Hatchett, *Commentary*, 551–52.

53. Phyllis Tickle, *The Divine Hours: Prayers for Summertime* (New York: Doubleday, 2000), x–xi).

54. Mitchell, *Praying Shapes Believing*, 49.

55. Ibid., 35.

56. Hatchett, *Commentary*, 138.

57. *The Rule of St. Benedict*, chapter 17.

58. Hymn 44 in *The Hymnal 1982*. Words: Latin, sixth century.

59. For a more extensive introduction to the church year, see my earlier book in this series, *Welcome to the Church Year: An Introduction to the Seasons of the Episcopal Church* (Harrisburg, PA: Morehouse Publishing, 2004).

60. Massey Shepherd Jr., *Liturgy and Education* (New York: Seabury Press, 1965), 98.

61. Joseph P. Russell, ed., *The New Prayer Book Guide to Christian Education*, rev. ed. (Cambridge, MA: Cowley Publications, 1996), xii.

62. Shepherd, *Liturgy and Education*, 100.

63. Dix, *Shape of the Liturgy*, 225. See the rubric in the 1979 Book of Common Prayer, 270.

64. Hatchett, *Commentary*, 237–38.

65. Ibid., 242.

66. Further information concerning the entire Journey to Adulthood program may be found at www.LeaderResources.org.

67. Quoted in Hatchett, *Commentary*, 435–36.

68. Price and Weil, *Liturgy for Living*, 200.

69. Hatchett, *Commentary*, 453.

70. Ibid., 472.

71. Marianne H. Micks, *The Joy of Worship* (New York: Church Publishing, 2004), 50.

72. Hatchett, *Commentary*, 556.

73. Mitchell, *Praying Shapes Believing*, 303.

74. Sydnor, *Prayer Book Through the Ages*, 123.

75. Ramsey, *Anglican Spirit*, 97.

76. Rebecca Lyman, *Early Christian Traditions*, vol. 6 of *The New Church's Teaching Series* (Cambridge, MA: Cowley Publications, 1999), 145.

77. Hatchett, *Commentary*, 584.

78. Lyman, *Early Christian Traditions*, 148.

79. Letter to Samuel Parker of Boston, quoted in Hatchett, *Commentary*, 585.

80. Massey H. Shepherd, *The Oxford American Prayer Book Commentary* (New York: Oxford University Press, 1950), 601.

81. Ramsey, *Anglican Spirit*, 97.

82. Ibid., 7.

83. Mitchell, *Praying Shapes Believing*, 278.